HOW A SHY GUY LIKE ME EARNED OVER

$1 MILLION IN NETWORK MARKETING

Without Selling, Phone Calls, Meetings or Any of That Other Stuff That Nobody Wants to Do

JOE BROWN
A FORMER "TEN-TIME LOSER"

**How A Shy Guy Like Me Earned Over
$1 MILLION IN NETWORK MARKETING
By Joe Brown**

Published by:
L & L Management
c/o 556 S. Fair Oaks, #101-169
Pasadena, California PZ [91105]
Fax: (626) 568-9165

Copyright © 2001 by Joe Brown

ISBN: 1-878873-00-8
Library of Congress Control Number: 00-91154

First Edition. All Rights Reserved.

No part of this publication may be reproduced, stored in an information retrieval system, or transmitted, in any form or by any means, electronic, mechanical, photocopying, recording, or otherwise, without prior written permission from the publisher.

Manufactured in the United States of America
1 2 3 4 5 6 7 8 9 10

Book and Cover Production by One-On-One Book Production, West Hills, California

Dedication

This book is dedicated to people like me—who tried and failed at network marketing and who thought they were too shy to succeed.

But who proved that success is possible when they learned the right approach for "the shy guy."

Disclaimer

Much of what you will read in this book is historical in nature and is not intended to fully represent current methods of network marketing in use by myself or the company with which I am affiliated. Neither Twin Labs nor any other company with which I am affiliated helped fund or write this book, nor do they endorse it in any way.

It is my wish that anyone reading my story fully understand that any marketing by its very nature is an ever-changing process affected by fluctuations in market forces, public whims and legal issues. This is a story of how "then" became "now." Many of the anecdotes I present are historical in nature and do not reflect the present network marketing methods in use by the company with which I am affiliated.

I have presented herein, to the best of my memory, a complete and accurate account of my struggles and triumphs. I have attempted to convey my own unique marketing methods and philosophy. It is my wish that this book will help you develop your own workable system and thus achieve those personal dreams of success you've had in your heart for so long.

Good luck and, I hope, good reading!

Special Thanks

Peter Harris who did such a great job of designing all my original fliers and advertisements and the original "Secrets" booklet. I am sure I would not have had the success I had without his amazing ability to take my ideas and represent them graphically on paper. Pete now designs web pages for Paul McCartney's step sister. Way to go Pete!

Phil Brown, my brother who kept my cassette business going when this business took off on me. I am proud to say I have never met a person with more integrity and just plain higher values than my brother Phil.

Barbara Wright, Frank Harvey and Mike Clutton who took over the leadership roles within the company when I was no longer able to do so.

Dick Hegle, my MLM friend who I continually bounced marketing ideas off of and was such a great encouragement to me. Here is another person with tremendous integrity.

Alan Vaughan, my friend and one of the best intuitives in the world who predicted almost five years earlier when I was flat broke that one day I would be a millionaire and write a book about my experiences.

Terry Paulson and Scotty Paulson who's ingenious idea of a totally different type of marketing plan that worked far beyond anyone's wildest expectations and changed the lives of thousands of people and made MLM history.

Joanne Nicoletti, for waiting on me night and day and taking care of me in my long-term illness and for being such a big and wonderful part of my life..

Skip Press, without whom this book would not be a reality.

About the Author

Joe Brown's formative years were spent in several locations in the southern United States: Washington, D.C.; Alexandria, Virginia; Clearwater, Florida; and finally in Morganton, North Carolina, the city where he was born. After finishing high school in Morganton, Joe attended Brevard College in North Carolina for two years, then did a two-year stint in the United States Marine Corps.

After military service, he moved to New England, living in Vermont and New Hampshire, working on a flood control dam, as a carpenter's helper, and cleaning ice and snow from rooftops in winter.

In the early days of computers he worked as a computer operator and also sold light bulbs. In 1973, Joe moved to California and returned to college at the ripe old age of 28. Unfortunately, he found his chosen degree was not too marketable, so he held jobs like popcorn machine repairman and apartment manager.

In 1985, he started his own seminar and conference audio recording company to provide on-site tape copies of popular talks. With this success, he began dabbling in network marketing, but had little luck in more than ten different companies. Standard multi-level marketing companies and the latest "hot" products had the same result; he would recruit few or no people, then drop out within a few months.

One day, Joe realized that the big network marketing successes were the natural, outgoing "born salesman" type. Basically an introvert, Joe wondered if he would ever achieve MLM success, but the potential monetary rewards were so appealing he didn't give up. Finally, he created a system to recruit people without the standard, bombastic, direct approach. In January of 1995, he refined his system into a mail order approach that enabled him to rise to the top of his company. This book is a chronicle of his winning ways.

Contents

Introduction 1

1. Find Something Different 7
2. The Real Route to Network Marketing Success 17
3. The Changes I Needed 29
4. My Secrets of Network Marketing Plans Revealed 53
5. Professional Sales = Network Marketing Success 77
6. How My System Evolved 101
7. Brainwash Yourself for Success 167
8. Maintaining Success 189
9. Seven Simple Steps to Sustained Success 197
10. Systems of the Future 221

Introduction

❚❚Hi. My name is Joe Brown, and in the last two years I've been in and out of about ten different network marketing companies. In each one I worked hard, gave it all I had and yet in every case I failed to have any success. In fact, I never received a check for more than $200 and most of the time I never made a cent and spent a whole lot more in marketing expenses than I received in return. Each time, I got further and further in the hole, and at the end of last year I said I would never get involved in a network marketing company again. And then I saw an ad about this company, and I was astonished at the simplicity of the marketing plan. I could see that finally, after 50 years of network marketing, someone finally came up with a way where the average person could start making money quickly, and not just the heavy hitters. I took a chance, and right now I'm amazed at what happened. My first check was $680, my second was $1,300, my third was $2,700 and my fourth check was over $5,000. I went from $0 to over $5,000 in four short months. I've never made money like this before. I'm so excited I'm about to jump out of my skin, and I have a hard time sleeping at night just thinking about it. I very realistically expect to be making $10,000 or more per month before the end of the year. I have people in my downline calling me, because they're finally making money when they've never made a cent before in network marketing. No matter how many times you've failed before in network marketing, please give this company just one more chance. It's changed my life and I believe it can change your life also."

The above two-minute phone message made more money for me and created a bigger splash in the world of network marketing than I ever thought was possible. Only one thing about it missed the mark. Instead of making $10,000 a month, it wasn't long before I was making $50,000 a month.

It's a good thing I created a steady income for myself, because I hit a point in my life where I was unable to work at all. This would have been a disaster for most self-employed persons, but in my case the money kept coming in. I was able to get by without worrying about my income.

How many people are able to do that?

At the urging of many friends and business associates, I resolved to tell my story. I wanted people like you to know about the first ten times I had failed in network marketing. I wanted folks to understand that I was almost 50 years old when I gave network marketing (sometimes called multi-level marketing, or MLM), one last chance. I wanted to explain how I now live in a nice house in an affluent neighborhood where I used to only walk through before, wistfully gazing up at the handsome estates I thought were out of my reach.

As I contemplated writing this book, I realized that if a quiet, shy guy like me, someone who doesn't like hard sell and never will, could introduce people to the simple, easily understood and workable secrets which helped me win, teaching the methods that anyone who can read and write can win with, I'd be helping my readers on the way to a dream.

Introduction

I'm enthusiastic now on a daily basis. Life is a lot different than it was when I walked back to my tiny apartment a few blocks away from the affluent neighborhood that I now live in. Despite my formerly modest circumstances and repeated failures at network marketing, I always felt that the average person did not make a success of network marketing because there was something missing in the programs they tried. The problem was, I didn't know what I was looking for; it was a case of "I'll know it when I see it." When I finally found a program that made sense and looked different than anything else I'd ever seen, I managed to work past my fears and trust my instincts one last time.

I didn't simply take it at face value, though. I called the owner of the company and asked a lot of questions.

I was pleased to discover that he was very open about how his company had been constructed. He told me the company planning was based on years of experience—his own and that of his father, who had supported their family with a network marketing business. Their new company sold good, legitimate, consumable products. He sounded honest, and he believed the methods he had devised might work, even though the structure favored distributors in a way that made traditional network marketing companies very nervous.

At the very least, he told me, it was a totally unique idea.

So I tried it, and I'm very glad I did.

There's a caveat to my story. My success did not come solely from the new company I found. I have determined that if people are not successful, a lot of the time it's because they don't believe in their own self-worth. It took me a while to realize that I had something to offer the world. My epiphany came when I got a check in the mail for $5,000 and realized that at that rate I was making $60,000 a year. That might not sound like much to some, but to me it was a fortune. At that point, I began to believe in something deeper than a marketing plan. I began to believe in myself, and that's made all the difference.

I'd like to help you do that, too. I have written this book to show you not only how to make a great part-time income in network marketing, but also to feel great about doing it.

Unlike me, you may not be a quiet, retiring person by nature. However, if you are, I feel this book will help you in two ways:

a. Tell you how to succeed in network marketing and

b. Help you allow yourself to believe you can get rich

You've probably heard the old saying: "I've been rich and I've been poor, and rich is better." That's only half the story. As I began to make substantial amounts of money, I began to realize how many other people I could help with my resources. Suddenly, the idea of being rich made a lot more sense. Since it's better to give than receive, I want to help you help others believe in themselves.

I intend to explain to you the best network marketing methods I've ever found. I hope you use them to successfully market any product which is well-suited to network marketing (not every product may be). I'll explain what worked for me, and then leave you to your own ideas. I'll also tell you what didn't work, and hopefully save you some of the wrong turns and dead-ends I took on the way to success.

Introduction

In this book I'll also cover the big lies told by some network marketing companies. I'll tell you how to create your own system of marketing, so that you don't feel like you're being squeezed into a cookie–cutter mold like you do with most network marketing companies. Drawing from my own experience and that of others, I'll take you step-by-step through an easily–understood plan that you can effortlessly explain to others so that they, too, can easily pass it on.

My intention is that you create a sustained success for yourself unlike anything you've ever accomplished.

Since I became the #1 sales person in my company, other companies have copied the methods I cover herein. Unlike most other companies, however, this one after five years, retains many of its distributors, which is phenomenal in the ever-changing world of network marketing. And when you're too busy trying to copy success, that leaves little time to think ahead and come up with new innovations.

This book isn't for copycats— it's for pacesetters.

Do you anticipate chapters about putting together meetings, holding training sessions, attending *rah–rah* conventions and convincing people to buy hundreds or thousands of dollars worth of product the first time you make a presentation?

Forget all that. I'll show you how I used ads, fliers, home-made booklets and audiotapes, unobtrusively left in public places or mailed to potential distributors, to recruit almost everyone in my downline. My #1 distributor, in fact, called me after finding one of my tapes in a public place.

If by now I have you interested, great. If not, I hope you do well elsewhere. Most likely, you're probably feeling like I did when I first heard about the plan I share in this book. You're probably still skeptical.

Whatever you are feeling, I hope you'll read further and find out how I learned to make $50,000 a month and more. If you're willing to read a few more pages, you might discover a new, better life.

1
FIND SOMETHING DIFFERENT

Network Marketing—What's True... And What's Not?

In my estimation, based on years of experience in network marketing, 90 percent of all distributors never see a check as big as $300. In fact, many people who venture into network marketing never recover their investment, and all they have to show for their initial enthusiasm are the products they bought to get them started. Nevertheless, I still believe that network marketing is the greatest single existing medium for the average person to become wealthy, starting with a relatively small investment.

If you've ever investigated network marketing, you may have heard some of the common rumors:

- ◆ Network marketing is taught at Harvard *(it's not in their catalog)*.

- ◆ Network marketing is illegal in some states *(not at this point)*.

- ◆ Network marketing is just another name for a pyramid scheme *(not true)*.

♦ 95 percent of network marketing companies never last two years.

On the latter point, a lot of companies come and go. On the other hand, the ones that have lasted the longest, such as Amway and Herbalife, make millionaires and great fortunes for their founders.

Will a Hot New Product Make You Rich?

As I mentioned in the introduction, I tried a number of network marketing companies over the years. I saw every kind of product and company structure imaginable, and failed with most of them until I came across the one that helped me become rich. There was one thing I remember hearing over and over with many companies:

"Just sell the product and the pay plan will take care of itself."

That statement is simply not true.

For any network marketing company to succeed, as with almost any business, the bulk of your income will come from repeat sales. Did you ever get a demonstration of a water filter, or buy one? How about the plastic-covered magnetic hockey puck looking "space age technology" thing that supposedly could replace using detergent in your washing machine?

I won't comment on either product, but I will say that there was a basic flaw with both those ideas. Once the customer made a purchase, it would be a long time before you would hear from them again, if you would ever hear from them.

I learned that you must look for a network marketing company that sells renewable products, meaning you'll get repeat business. Think about it. I mentioned two highly successful companies above—Amway and Herbalife.

The first became famous for the soap its distributors sold, while the other gained its reputation on vitamins and herbs. With success, each company expanded its product catalog, almost completely with renewable products. So that's my first advice to you in selecting any network marketing company—find one that sells high quality, renewable products that people will use and keep using on a regular basis, hopefully for the rest of their lives.

When I found the company that finally worked for me, I'd personally been through all the old sales pitches, and struck out every time. One thing I was certain of was that I couldn't just concentrate on selling the products and let the pay plan take care of itself.

The products had to be good, renewable products, ***but if the company pay plan was not structured to be friendly to new distributors coming onboard, it would eventually be self-defeating.*** Due to my own unique personal situation, any new company I investigated had to be something I could succeed at via methods that suited my own particular personality.

The Road to Riches I Almost Missed

Most stories of successful people generally fit into two categories: (a) those who became successful at a young age; and (b) older people whom have lost their fortune several times, only to win it back. My story is a little different. I had been broke all my life, until I found the company with which I made a fortune. At the age of 50, I was living and working out of a two-bedroom apartment where I had been for the past eight years. I drove an old car with the fender smashed in. In 1992, I was forced to declare bankruptcy. At no time in my life had I ever had more than two or three thousand dollars in the bank.

For the longest time, my story was typical of anyone who believed in the basic concept of network marketing but had never made a success of it. I had been in and out of various companies for years. Time after time, I followed the common pattern of recruiting one or two people and then dropping out in a month or two, often spending more money than I had earned.

Nevertheless, I came across several successful network marketers, and they each had a simple, common denominator: they were effective because they were natural–born sales-people. They had the gift of gab and were not afraid to give a sales pitch to anyone. These "Type A" personalities were very outgoing and friendly and had no problem using what is known in network marketing as "the three foot rule." By that I mean you go down the street with your business card, your sample product or whatever you're selling, and to anyone who comes within three feet you say something like: "How would you like to feel great and make money at the same time?" How would you like to do that? Unfortunately, most people cannot or will not take that approach.

I had to come up with another way of promoting my business that suited my personality. I wanted to build my downline—the people I recruited into the program—in a way I call "the shy guy approach." I wanted to recruit distributors via mailings and advertising.

It made sense to me, but every network marketer I'd ever mentioned the idea to told me it was impossible.

The three-foot rule did not suit my personality. I could simply never bring myself to do it. Even today, with all my success, I still do not approach people well. Because of this, I knew that if I was ever going to be successful in network marketing I would have to come up with a way to promote with what I call my "shy guy" approach. Despite most people telling me such a method would never fly, I had worked hard in several programs at creating such a system.

I finally had some success with one company because they had a good audiotape, but their compensation plan was a "breakaway." As soon as individuals under me got to the top level, their checks went down instead of up. As a result, they became discouraged and stopped working. And who could blame them? It was very frustrating for all of us.

Then, in 1994, I went to a seminar put on by a network marketing company that was doing very well. Despite the fact that they had only one product, they were growing rapidly. To my surprise, they spent most of their time talking about their pay plan, rather than their hot product. I'd never seen a company do this. Many of the leaders of their company had worked hard at other programs, but with little success. When they got into this new, one-product program, however, they started making good money. This company looked like the end of the rainbow, but it was only the calm following the storm.

Ultimately, this company did not work for me because it was structured so that you had to recruit ten people into your downline before you could cover your own required monthly purchase. I worked this program and recruited about ten people, only to have most of them drop out within a few months because they could not get into profit. It was another disappointment, but I gained something new and important. For the first time, I realized what truly determines the success of any network marketing company. For this reason alone, the experience was a real eye–opener.

I Find the Real Key to Success

In January of 1995, I saw an ad in a network-marketing magazine that changed my life forever. This company's ad was not focused on a hot "revolutionary" product. The company's basic orientation was so different from other network marketing companies I wondered how it could be possible. The funny thing is, I'd seen their ad before, at least once, maybe two or three times before, yet I had never bothered to read what it had to say. What caught my eye this time was not the headline, but the second line, the sub–head:

> **"NOW YOU CAN MAKE REAL MLM MONEY WITHOUT HAVING A LARGE NUMBER OF DISTRIBUTORS!"**

This idea appealed to me greatly, but nagging doubts based on past failures threatened to consume me. I had recently promised myself that I was through losing money and my network marketing days were over. I was just about ready to give up my dream and be "realistic." Still, something deep inside reminded me that it takes years to learn how to succeed at something. I knew that you can learn by experience, and that learning includes failure. More specifically, I'd observed another common quality about successful network marketers. They all had superior salesmanship, but they were also all willing to fail.

No doubt about it, I was a big success at failing! I failed many times, but very few people I'd ever met had been able to quit their job and become an overnight success in network marketing. No successful network marketer I'd ever known was afraid to fail. You had to be willing to fail; I knew that fully. You fail, you figure out what you can learn from the experience, you pull yourself up by your bootstraps, and you go on.

Unfortunately, there was no college course available on network marketing. Sure, there was some very good material available for people who were new to the subject, but network marketing education mostly boiled down to experience and practice. You tried one time and you did it over and over, and through the years, you developed a knack for it.

That was my understanding, anyway. So when I looked at this ad for the second or third time and the line caught my eye, I read every word. I looked at it and I looked at it some more and my eyes started to widen. I grabbed my calculator and started figuring, and after about ten minutes I said, "Wow, this is incredible!" If what I was reading was real, it answered many of the problems that I've been dealing with for the past several years with regard to distributor dropout and things like that. I wondered if they had actually discovered some secret success formula that I'd always suspected might exist.

I was so excited about the potential, I had a hard time sleeping. With this new structure I was reading about, I immediately saw that with only three people working in my downline, I could break even on my initial investment. If this is a real thing, I thought, this is going to do very well.

I called the company the next day. To my surprise, the owner answered the phone. I asked him several questions about his own experience and the uniqueness of the structure that I had read about in the ad. He seemed genuine, and down to earth. I felt like I could trust him. He told me the company was founded and financed solely by him and his father. He'd begun his own networking experience at a nutritional company over 20 years before. In the last program he and his father had been involved in, the father had been national marketing director. He described their new company, and elaborated further on his leadership experience.

"We came up with the concept you responded to after evaluating our past experiences in network marketing companies," he explained. "In designing this program we looked back to see what didn't work in the companies that we were previously associated with. We came to the conclusion that a lot of the programs out there, including some of the ones we were involved in, had a marketing or compensation program that actually stacked the odds against the average distributor succeeding. There were low commission payouts in the beginning and you had to build the network marketing organization."

He paused when he heard me laugh. I told him I'd been through the exact scenario that he was taking great pains to describe.

"We found that there was this large revolving door where we'd have hundreds of people joining our organization in a given month, and a hundred or so people dropping out," he continued, then waited while I chuckled again. "We determined that the average distributor does not have the financial resources to support his business for three or four or six months until his organization grows to reach the qualifying parameters that will keep his business going. We realized that a person can only work so hard so long without making any money, and then they drop along the wayside." He paused before adding, "I don't know if you experienced that yourself, Joe?"

"I understand 100 percent what you're talking about," I said quietly.

"Great. So basically in a nutshell we created this program so that the average distributor would be allowed to make several thousand dollars a month with a total downline base of only 30 to 50 distributors. The program is structured realistically. You know about the old way of doing it, where you had to have several hundred distributors to make several hundred dollars a month? We've kind of flipped everything backwards. We're immediately rewarding every single distributor when he comes into the business, when he starts sponsoring people, and when he starts building his organization. We're not going to wait to reward him after he's worked real hard and brought a lot of people into the business. That's really what our company is all about."

He told me about more complex aspects built into the system, but I didn't pay much attention to that. I didn't expect to ever make much money as a leading distributor. I did that later, but at the time I still wasn't convinced it was possible. I was simply impressed by the way I could recover my initial investment quickly and start making a profit, and I knew I could promote that concept to others that had been through similar struggles as mine.

Although we talked for some time longer, I'd heard enough to convince me that this was a company I wanted to try. The ad looked good, the figures added up, the owner of the company answered the phone personally, and he didn't seem to be in any hurry to get off the phone or reluctant to answer any question I posed. I had no way of knowing the program was going to take off like it did. In some ways, it was just one of many other things that I'd gotten into, but because of this new marketing plan, I was certain I would be able to recruit people quite easily. I believed, without standing in the mirror and giving myself rah–rah speeches, that because the company structure was so good I wouldn't have any trouble getting people in.

Every book I had ever read on success told me that the most important ingredient is expecting to have happen what you want to happen. And I did expect to get people in because of that marketing plan. That alone was enough to get me past any nagging, negative thoughts about past failures. On the other hand, I promised myself that if this plan didn't work out, I was finished with network marketing for good.

The next day I signed up, and my future was changed forever. I had found the rainbow and I was on the path to the pot of gold. I didn't know that then, or get there immediately, but I was so enthused with possibilities I knew I would not—as I had with some other programs—get discouraged if the first few people that I recruited did not turn out to be real dynamos who would work as hard as I did.

I was lucky enough to get in on the ground floor of a company that changed network marketing forever by offering a unique pay structure that transformed the lives of thousands of individuals who, like me, had only previously dreamed of success.

Or maybe it wasn't luck. Maybe I'd paid my dues, suffered my failures, and it was merely fitting that I had found the right program at last. In any event, I don't think any of us had any idea just how successful we were all about to become. The changes would be nothing short of amazing.

2
THE REAL ROUTE TO NETWORK MARKETING SUCCESS

If you have some experience with network marketing but have not yet made a success of it, you might be suffering from some common misconceptions, which usually come from bad information. I feel like I've seen them all, so I wanted to blow some holes in some of the "conventional wisdom" about network marketing, and then lay out some rules that I believe will help anyone in pursuing success in this field, whether they be rookies or veterans. Let's start with the things that don't work for me.

Don't Believe Everything You Hear

Most network marketing companies will tell you to sit down and write out the names of all the friends and family you think you might be able to get involved in your new business. That was not easy for me, because I always kept to myself and didn't talk to family and friends that much. So my list wasn't very extensive. I'm just not a gregarious guy, or at least I wasn't in those earlier days.. When I did make attempts to talk to family and friends about network marketings, it didn't take me long to discover they simply weren't interested. Even today, when I make as much money in a month as some of them do in a year, they are still not interested! I stopped trying to figure out why a long time ago. I've decided you're either inclined to becoming an entrepreneur, or you're not.

Being unobtrusive and unassuming has always been my nature. I've never been one to crow about what I'm doing, good or bad, to friends and family. I guess that some time in my childhood I formed the opinion that if I did something great, they wouldn't believe me, anyway. (Remember what I told you about getting over negative ideas of self-worth?) Naturally, you have to toot your own horn a little when you send out newsletters to distributors, or when you write a book like this. What I'm talking about here is how I generally have acted in one on one situations, which is quiet and shy.

Don't take my word about my failings. Here's a testimonial from my friend Pete Harris. He explains my experience better than I can:

"I have been working with Joe on and off for about the last three years, designing flyers and sending out mailings for him. I've seen Joe get involved with nearly a dozen network marketing companies and wished he hadn't, because I watched him lose money every time. I used to think he was crazy for jumping into so many programs. When he found the right company and took off, I saw checks start rolling in that amazed me. $670, $1300, $2700, $5000,

$7500... all the way up to the latest whopper of $21,000! I just have to say, it's all true." Of course, the checks have grown larger since Pete wrote that for me, but I hope you get the point. I did it my own quiet way. If you join a network marketing company and think you have to transform yourself into the world's greatest speaker, or become the kind of person who could run a cheerleading summer camp, you could be buying into a lie. You have to find a way to reach people that suits your own unique personality.

THE BIG LIE! (Just Sell the Product and the Pay Plan Will Take Care of Itself)

With any network marketing company I ever tried, I felt good about my prospects, or I wouldn't have pursued the program. I also continually came across a mantra that I began to feel was a fact of life, at least for network marketers:

"Just sell the product and the pay plan will take care of itself."

Why did people say this? Or believe this? It's very simple. Most pay plans are complex, and structured to heavily favor the owners of the company and those folks who get started with the company early on. Some programs are like Ponzi or pyramid schemes, set up to make a lot of money fast for those who get involved first. After a while, the company goes belly-up and these people disappear, leaving the latest arrivals in the lurch.

When things like this happen, it gives all of network marketing a bad name. If people believe they're selling a great product, however, something truly worthwhile that might not be available elsewhere, it's easy to get them enthusiastic and have that wave of enthusiasm carry forward. Most people have trouble balancing their checkbooks, much less understanding complex network marketing compensation plans. So when you tell them the product is good and to just sell that and let the pay plan take care of itself, they're happy to believe it. After all, isn't the person telling them this driving a nice car, and dressed nicely? Appearances are reality, aren't they?

You and I both know that's not always true. Nevertheless, I always heard "Just sell the product and the pay plan will take care of itself" again and again, and again and again it never did.

I heard this kind of pitch from "heavy hitters" who have downlines of distributors who follow them from company to company. It took me a while to realize that the big checks they waved in my face were not realistic representations of what an average person starting from scratch could obtain. Here's some examples of my network marketing failures. I won't mention names, but the false starts might sound familiar to you:

- Company #1: I spent a thousand dollars in advertising and marketing over a period of three months and recruited 13 people, resulting in one check for $155.

- Company #2: I worked for years with this program and never received a check for more than $200.

- Company #3: Three months work resulted in no check.

- Company #4: I worked for several months, recruited some people, and the company stopped paying!

- Company #5: No check after several months' work.

- Company #6: I did a lot of mailings for two months, and got no check. I don't want to even think about what I spent on postage.

- Company #7: Never made more than $100.

- Company #8: I never made more than $10 a month.

- Company #9: Although I was in on it at the beginning, I never got a check for more than $100.

There are more, but they're irrelevant—the ones listed above are the good ones!

I hope I've made it clear by now that every network marketing company I touched did not turn to gold. I lost at most, and spent more money promoting than I care to think about. It should also be obvious that I did not build up a giant downline that followed me blindly from program to program.

In 1994, I went to a seminar by a network marketing company that was doing very well. They had only one product, and the company was growing rapidly. Simple, easy to understand. Many of the people who were successful at this company had worked hard at other programs but with little success. When they got into this program, with only one product to sell, they started making good money.

The seminar was a real eye-opener.

Problematically, the company did not work for me, because you still needed around ten people in your downline before you could cover your required monthly purchase. I worked the program for a few months, recruited about ten people, and then was disappointed once again as most of them dropped out when they could not get into profit. It was yet another example of how the pay plan will not take care of itself if you simply concentrate on selling the product, even if you sell only one great product.

In contrast to my experience with that company is the company where I made my fortune, where many new distributors are in profit within three months. Some distributors also make $200 to $300 their first month.

What's the norm? Only the "hitters" earn the high percentages in most companies. While they claim a "potential" payout of 55–60 percent, their actual payout ends up being around 25–27 percent.

Similarly, the average distributor retention rate for most network marketing companies after a year is a measly 15 percent, which means they lose 85 percent of everyone who joins. What kind of company is that?

Most people fail in network marketing because they get sold on a product or service but do not realize they are getting ripped off by their company's marketing plan or some other aspect stacks the odds against the new distributor.

When a network marketing company tells you about a "potential" payout, you need to ask how many people are actually receiving that potential payout. In my experience, unless you are an experienced, professional network marketer you will never come close to that "potential" payout. The only thing that counts for you is what the company pays out to its distributors "on average."

The company that I settled on has an actual payout of more than 60 percent, which is twice the industry average. The seventh largest CPA firm in the United States confirmed that the company's distributor retention rate was an astonishing 75 percent over two years. This type of retention was previously unheard of in network marketing. Any mathematician or professional gambler will tell you it's always better to go where the odds are in your favor.

More on all that later. Now let's cover some of the other network marketing lies that are out there.

The Big Name Star Doesn't Know Your Name
FIND OUT WHERE
THE BIG GUNS ARE GOING
But don't go there!

Let's say you've been hearing about a new network marketing company where people are making tons of money and changing their lives. We'll call it Acme Vitamins. Acme offers very professional-looking promotional material, and they're happy to send it to you. So there you are, sitting on your couch, watching a flashy video on which Acme spokesperson Fred Former Footballplayer smiles and says the world will flock to your door to buy these products and join your downline with hardly any effort! That's how revolutionary this product is! And here come the testimonials:

"Why yes, Fred, you wouldn't believe how easy it is. Wow!"

"Fred, I didn't believe it until I tried it, and then my biggest problem was not getting trampled when people stampeded over to my house to sign up!"

It never works that way, but people will believe that "pitch" day after day. After you study network marketing for a time, you realize that Fred Former Footballplayer seems to like a lot of companies, maybe a lot more than make sense, unless he's getting paid to shill for these companies. Chances are very good that Fred Former Footballplayer has never tried the products, and certainly wouldn't know your name if you met him at a convention.

Network marketing, like any business, takes time to learn. Like most distributors, I spent years chasing the golden dream of a lucrative, substantial income through network marketing. I read thousands of ads and listened to and watched dozens of tapes. Each ad and tape promised the same thing—a successful part-time business if you would only join their program. They had it all figured out, and presented it in a way that made you feel like you simply could not lose. Each time I tried a program and failed, I learned a little more about what does not work. Believe me—celebrity endorsements really do not matter to most people who will buy your products or get involved with your company.

Your Attitude Toward Failure

I've found that what most people really want to achieve out of network marketing is simple. They want a business they can work from their home. No more freeway traffic jams, no more alarm clocks, no more unappreciative bosses. And best of all, no more living from paycheck to paycheck. These days, the average person has roughly two options: (a) come up with a single big payday to set you up, such as an invention, winning the lottery or some other windfall; or (b) get into a network marketing company where you have to go to sales meetings, learn a canned sales pitch to give to all your friends and relatives, and start working part–time while holding down a full–time job. Usually, if you choose (b) it also requires you to outlay a substantial amount of money up front to load up on the products the network marketing company is selling. And if (b) doesn't work out, you have a garage full of Goodwill donations.

I could give you an example here of a generic bad/normal network marketing structure. Something for the aforementioned fictional Acme Vitamins, perhaps, but it might only serve as a distraction or confusion. What is more important at this point are basic principles of network marketing, what works and what does not.

For years, I was an "opportunity seeker," which is a polite name for "sucker." While I chased my dreams, I had a full-time job, taping lectures at conventions and duplicating and distributing those tapes. One of the events I worked regularly was the Whole Life Expo in California. I listened to all sorts of speakers there, everything from proponents of healing crystals to more mainstream folks like Deepak Chopra, the doctor who combined ancient Aryuvedic philosophy with Occidental medicine to create a whole new way of thinking about health.

Although I got "taken for a ride" many, many times by network marketing companies, I kept sensing that there was a way to make a fortune in network marketing, and the positive thinkers I would encounter at Whole Life Expo helped convince me that to be a success you have to pick yourself up and start over again, no matter how many times you fall. Rather than wallowing in your pain and failures, you have to discern the essential lesson that can be learned from each and every experience, positive or negative.

So now that I've told you some of the things to avoid in network marketing companies, allow me to sum up some things to look for in choosing a network marketing company that will work for you and allow you to achieve that dream of a business you can work out of your home to build the wealth you've always desired for yourself and those you love.

Lesson #1

One of the most common mistakes new network marketers (and even experienced ones) make is believing that someone else is going to do all of the work and build your downline for you. I have never met, talked to or ever even heard of anyone who ended up earning a substantial income in a program where they did nothing but mail out postcards. Sure, some received checks, but no one is going to make real, substantial, residual income by simply mailing out postcards. I used my own "quiet guy" system, which I'll explain in detail later, but I did more than mail out postcards.

With any company, you have to keep your thinking cap on. If someone says they are going to build your downline for you, as their group gets bigger they will need to find more and more people for each person they recruit. After all, those folks need a downline, too. After a while, your "do it all" upline cannot keep on bringing in five to ten more new distributors for the last one they recruited. It simply does not work out, mathematically or realistically. If you are serious about making a good income in network marketing, you need to realize that it takes personal, continuous effort on your part. Network marketing is a business, not a get rich quick scheme. The big checks come from hard work.

Lesson #2

Do not get into any network marketing program unless you fully understand how the pay plan works. It is my personal belief that most network marketing pay plans are designed to confuse the new distributor, because it's easier to ask a confused person to buy a substantial amount of product when they enter the program. Don't ever believe the line "just sell the product and the money will take care of itself."

You might as well say a prayer to the tooth fairy.

The company that made me rich enables a distributor to get into profit with three people. I like to compare it to gears on a car. The first two get you moving, and the third one gives you speed. The first two levels of the company structure enable you to get into profit quickly, while the "leadership bonus" (I'll explain later) is where you make the big money. The money distributors earn from the first few checks of this program comes almost entirely from the first two levels. As you progress, 80 percent of the check amounts can be derived from the leadership bonus. Most importantly, however, any normal person can understand how the pay plan works.

Lesson #3

When considering a network marketing program, ask this question:

"Does your sponsor have a duplicatable system?"

By this I mean, can you explain it to others as easily as it is explained to you? If your sponsor or upline is making big bucks by using his or her natural ability to talk on the phone, and you don't share this "gift of gab," this is not a duplicatable system. If someone gets you on the phone and pumps you up about how much money they and all their buddies are making, can you and your future downline do that very same thing? If not, they do not have a duplicatable system and you are probably going to lose by attempting to use it.

Since I realized that most people do not like to sell or work the phones, I created a fully duplicatable three-step system that any potential distributor can understand and bring others to understand easily. You should settle for nothing less.

Lesson #4

Here is the most important point of all. You need to find out what percentage of the distributors in your potential company are really making money. Every company has its stars, but what about the average person? If you are thinking about getting into a new program, ask your sponsor or upline what percentage of all the distributors are actually making a profit. Press them further, and ask for real figures. My bet is that they will give you some excuse why they won't tell you. I now make more money than I ever dreamed possible. What is more important is this—I am a part of a company that has a tremendously high percentage of average people making good money.

I was able to get rich not at the expense of my distributors, but because of their success. Now that is something I am really happy about, and I don't mind giving anyone real figures.

And now I'm going to tell you all about that company, and why it worked for me when so many others did not. With this company, I finally found the elusive formula for success I kept thinking was out there. I believe you'll find my story heartening.

3
THE CHANGES I NEEDED

Until now, I've been vague about the company that enabled me to finally fulfill the promise of network marketing I had always felt was there, the promise I'd never found. It is not the purpose of this book to be a sales or recruiting tool for any particular company. However, it is impossible for me to give a complete historical record of my success without going into some detail about the company that made it all possible and how the unique structure of this company played a crucial role in my success. The company that helped me realize my dream is Changes International. It was January of 1995 when I saw their ad in Cutting Edge magazine and the sub-head that caught my eye:

"NOW YOU CAN MAKE REAL MLM MONEY WITHOUT HAVING A LARGE NUMBER OF DISTRIBUTORS!"

I came to Changes early, as MLM companies go. The company was only six months old when I joined, but in the first year they ballooned to thousands of distributors. Their success subsequently snowballed. They are expanding into Canada and the United

Kingdom, and both the buying public and network marketing pros have taken notice.

The company's rapid success and reputation for excellence was so dramatic they gained the notice of TWINLAB, an internationally respected nutritional supplement company which has been in existence for three decades. TWINLAB President and CEO Ross Blechman was so impressed with Changes he bought the company and promptly invested thousands in software and hardware to make Changes as technologically-advanced as any MLM in the business. Changes International changed my life forever, but I'm not alone. They also changed the history of network marketing forever. Here, in a nutshell, is the program that did it.

The Changes Story

Changes International was co-founded by its president and CEO, Scott Paulsen, and his father, Terry Paulsen. The name of the company is an acronym for Continuing Health And Nutrition Gives Everyone Strength, which sums up the company philosophy. As I've mentioned, I was not actively looking to get involved with another program when I found Changes International.

All right, I know what you're thinking. If I wasn't interested, why was I reading an ad in an MLM magazine? Maybe there was some interest on my part, but it was a tiny little apathetic glimmer of hope that might have died away forever if I had not gotten involved with Changes. When I read that ad, I grabbed my calculator and did some figuring, and after about ten minutes I said "Wow, this is incredible!" I said it out loud, to myself. That's how impressed I was. The ad alone answered so many of the problems that I had been dealing with, such as distributor dropout rates. I was so excited about the prospects of Changes, I had a hard time sleeping that night.

The next morning I called the company and got through to Scott Paulsen immediately. The reason I mention this is that no one called me about this company. Even though I wasn't actively pursuing network marketing prior to reading the Changes ad, I still got calls all the time from people trying to get me into programs. When I saw the Changes ad and understood how revolutionary their marketing plan was for the average distributor, I had to call. I just couldn't believe it.

> **NOTE:** *In the following discussion with Changes co-founder Scott Paulsen, the term "infinity bonus" is used. This was the term in use at the time I joined the company. After Changes International merged with Twin Labs, this term was replaced by "leadership bonus," which is the term used today.*

I was impressed that Scott took my call personally, and seemed in no hurry to get off the phone. Here's what he told me about his background and why he and his father decided to start Changes International.

Terry Paulsen began his networking experience at a nutritional company in the late 70s, and gained two decades of experience succeeding in other programs. Immediately prior to starting Changes, both he and Scott were involved in a company where Terry served as national marketing director. They decided one day to pool their successes, experience and leadership capabilities to build their own program. Scott had a successful business background both in network marketing and traditional companies. The Paulsens simply got so tired of working for others they decided to take a risk, getting advances on their credit cards to create Changes International. The company opened its doors in July of 1994.

"We came up with the concept after evaluating our past experiences in network marketing companies," Scott told me. "In designing this program we looked back to see what didn't work in the programs that we were previously associated with. We came to a conclusion that a lot of the programs that are out there, including some of the ones that we were involved in, had a marketing or compensation program that actually stacked the odds against the average distributor succeeding. Specifically, you had to build the network marketing organization despite low commission payouts in the beginning.

"We found that there was this large revolving door where we'd have hundreds of people joining our organization in a given month, and a hundred or so people dropping out."

I'd seen that, too, so I asked Scott what he and Terry thought was the reason behind such a drop off rate, when such large sums of money were promised on the back end of every program.

"We determined that the average distributor does not have the financial resources to support his business for three or four or six months until his organization grows to the lower levels of the pay plan," he answered, "until he reaches the qualifying parameters that the compensation plan might have. We realized that a person can only work so hard so long without making any money, and then they drop along the wayside."

Anyone who had been in network marketing for any length of time, successful or otherwise, had been hit smack in the face with that reality. I understood 100 percent what Scott was talking about.

"Basically, we created this program so that the average distributor would be allowed to make several thousand dollars a month with a total distributor base of 30 to 50 people," Scott explained. "The old way of doing it was that you had to have several hundred distributors to make several hundred dollars a month. We flipped everything backwards to reward every single distributor who comes into the business immediately when he starts sponsoring people and building his organization. We didn't want to wait to reward him after he's worked real hard and brought a lot of people into the business. That's really what Changes International is all about."

I knew exactly what he meant. I told Scott I'd had that experience over and over, getting into a new program, working really hard for a month or two and then, when I didn't get some little bit of money to give me some incentive, I just said the heck with it and gave up.

Scott commiserated with me. "In our evaluations before designing Changes, we had databases from previous marketing ventures that we were in, with anywhere from 4,000 to 8,000 people. In evaluating those results we realized that percentage-wise, we had more people on the fourth, fifth, sixth, seventh level. We saw that if we were to take the totals of the amount of people on each level, the ratio of active distributors purchasing and participating in the business were grouped right up against where my Dad and I were, at the first and second level. We concluded that the reason we made it to the first or second level was that we were good network marketers and we communicated well with our first and second level people. Communication. That's where really building a network marketing organization starts. It's your base, it's your foundation, and it's where your most activity is going to be ratio-wise."

Scott got into numbers. He told me that if I had 100 people on a 6th level who weren't well–supported by their 1st and 2nd level, I might find that only 50 percent or 25 percent of those 100 people on the 6th level were actually active in any particular month. In the early stages of Changes International, however, 95 percent of their 1st and 2nd and 3rd level people were active.

"The ratios of active distributors dropped in every single program scenario that we looked at," Scott said. "The further it went down, the active versus inactive ratio went down. So we designed a two-level marketing plan where people can communicate and get paid off the largest percentage active distributor ratio possible."

He gave me an example. If I worked the Changes program long enough to bring six people into the business and communicate with them and help them get four distributors each, I would be in a position to make $15 on all 6 first level people and $45 each on the 24 people on my second level who came from those six first level distributors.

In other words, I would have a total of 30 distributors that I brought into the business, which would earn me around $1200 a month in commission and also qualify me for Changes' 4 percent third level through leadership bonus for any activity on my third level down.

"That's powerful," Scott said. "That $1200 a month will change a lot of people's lives. That's an extra $13,000 to $14,000 a year. And that's based on 30 distributors, not 300 or 1,000. It's achievable. When we came out with this, a lot of people started to realize that they could really make decent money."

Scott went on to explain what he called the "super-recruiter scenario" which he projected was

The Changes I Needed

possible after a year's work. His idea was for me to bring in one good distributor per month for the whole year, giving me 12 distributors on my first level. Then, throughout the year, I would help these 12 get 8 distributors each. That would give me a total of 108 distributors on my first and second level after a year. Based on those distributors merely staying active, my monthly commission would then be in excess of $4,500 on those 108 people on my first and second level alone. Plus, I would be paid an up to 8 percent third level to infinity bonus on my third, fourth, seventh, 10th, 20th level all the way down through the organization.

"So really there's a massive amount of money to be made in this marketing plan," Scott enthused.

If you've never been involved in a network marketing program before, the above explanation might be a bit confusing. Not nearly as complicated as all the other programs I was involved in before Changes, but if you don't understand what Scott was saying, please read it over again. I believe you'll understand it fairly easily, because that's what Scott and Terry intended. (I also explain it in detail later in this book.)

Success with their program was much more attainable than some of the others I'd seen, where you had to go so deep in levels of distributors, getting so many hundreds and hundreds of people in your downline before you could make any meaningful profit. I shared with Scott some of the frustrations I'd had with previous network marketing company pay plans.

"Yeah, with some programs, before you can get to the next level or plateau, your group has to do $5,000." He knew exactly what I had been through. "So you sit stagnant, dependent on what everybody else does. In this program you're dependent on what you do.

Whatever you do and you produce you're going to get paid on. You're not going to have to sit back and hope that the people you put into the business do a certain amount of volume so that you can qualify for your checks. You dictate how much money you're going to make in a two–level program like this."

I asked Scott to give me some specific figures on what it took to qualify each month. How much product did I have to buy to remain active? (With all network marketing programs I've ever seen you have to buy a certain "qualifying" amount of any product each month to qualify for bonuses.)

"Any combination of six bottles of product is what's considered a six–pack," he said. "It's $16.67 a bottle, which comes out to $100. So the monthly purchase is a $100 six–pack to qualify for your bonuses, OK? What that allows you to do is collect 15 percent on your first level and 45 percent on your second level."

> **NOTE:** *There have been some price changes since I first became involved in the company; the prices above were current when I first interviewed Scott.*

Well, what do you know? He had explained the pay plan first, then started talking about the products. Wasn't this refreshing—someone running a network marketing company who would admit that people got into network marketing because they wanted to make money, not to change the world with self–styled wonder products.

I did relatively well in one other network marketing company, reaching the upper stages, but I still didn't make much money. As a result, I never truly understood how these complex pay plans worked. With Changes, the philosophy was that whatever you

The Changes I Needed

do and produce you get paid on. That simple philosophy held throughout the program.

"For the distributors who come in and work the program and build an organization and help people," he explained, "we offer the infinity bonus. This program basically goes in four stages and is based on the amount of distributors you bring into the business. Now keep in mind your distributor cost is still the same, $100 per month for six bottles of the product. When you bring three people into the business, that's going to put you in a position to make up to a 4 percent payout third level through infinity bonus. The next stage would be six personally-sponsored distributors. As soon as you have these six personally-sponsored distributors, your third level to infinity bonus jumps to 8 percent. When you build your business to nine personally-sponsored distributors, that boosts your third level to infinity bonus to 12 percent. And the final stage that you would ever have to achieve would be twelve personally–sponsored first level distributors, which will pay you up to a 15 percent third level to infinity bonus. And that, if you were to sit down and run the numbers, can be real powerful."

I hadn't run all the numbers, but I could see it could really add up.

The main reason I thought the Changes structure was so much more attainable was because people on any level only had to be concerned with the two levels of distributors under them. Anyone could see this was a much more easily managed structure. In many programs I'd tried, there was some type of upper level bonus, but it was way, way out of reach for the normal distributor. The upper level payouts of the Changes program were much more attainable for the average person. The other programs out there also paid a much lower percentage when a distributor reached their maximum bonus, anywhere between 1 percent and 5 percent.

Scott said the "normal" infinity bonuses offered had gone into their calculations. "We're offering a situation where you could technically develop 12 first level legs of your organization and basically be collecting 15 percent on a third, fourth, fifth level," he said. "So for the person who really builds his business and goes out and qualifies as a four-star executive, which is 12 personally–sponsored distributors, as your distributors grow on the third, fourth, fifth levels, you have the opportunity to make up to 15 percent on those levels. The amount of money you can make is incredible."

I didn't want to think about the big money in my first phone conversation with Scott. After all, no matter how good Changes sounded, I'd never made the kind of money he was projecting, and I'm not sure if I thought it was possible. I didn't know that I would ever get twelve distributors working under me, but I did know that, even if I only got one person into the program per month there was a good chance I might attain something near the type of success Scott had plotted out. Plus, he carefully explained to me how the attrition rate of Changes distributors was much, much lower than average.

"So the people that you get involved are going to stay in rather than drop out," he stressed. "In the total distributor base of our company, we have a significantly higher activity rate than most companies. Other companies feel they can brag about their success even though they have a substantially lower activity ratio than ours. What that boils down to, and what a lot of people don't understand, is that we have many of our distributors reordering every month.

The Changes I Needed

What that really means, Joe, is that we have a very extremely low distributor dropout. The higher your distributor retention rate is, the more distributors are making money. Even if a distributor in his first month in the business can come in and make $40 or $80 or $100 in addition to getting back his original investment, he's there, making money from Day One. And if distributors are making money they're going to hang with the program."

How could I argue? I knew from talking to people in network marketing that if they could just get a check, even though it might be small by a lot of people's standards, it would encourage them to keep on working. It didn't have to be a gigantic check, just some positive cash flow. And with the high amount of people staying in the company, I wouldn't be stepping onto the same old treadmill, recruiting 10 and then having 7 or 8 drop out, and then recruiting 10 more. The recruiting treadmill was a really worrisome, discouraging thing.

I was becoming convinced, and I suppose Scott knew it, because he began explaining the products to me. Despite their concentration on perfecting the pay plan, he and Terry had paid close attention to the quality of the products, down to minute ingredients.

"We have two of the absolutely most hottest products on the market: Thermolift, an all-herbal energizer and fatburner, with patented chromium piccolinate. A lot of distributors in the field have had tremendous, tremendous luck with the Thermolift product. In our past experience, we marketed an energizer type of product, so we're very familiar with the formulations and the testimonials and that was why we elected to bring out Thermolift. You can give a sample to somebody and get an emotional involvement in the product almost immediately after trying it. Our

Performax product, which is a powerful super antioxidant formula, has had massive exposure in the market. What we're putting in it is maritime pine bark extract and OPC85 plus grape seed extract. We have an even combination. We've got 25 milligrams of each product. There's been some tremendous testimonials, but we can't really go into any of the medical benefits that people have experienced from any of our products because we're not medical doctors."

I was particularly interested in the third product he described, colloidal silver. The 4 oz. bottle sold by Changes was a five parts per million silver/water solution. My friend explained the product had been around a long time, was used extensively during wartime, had a lot of helpful benefits, and was making a comeback. The distributor cost was only $16.67. I was familiar with colloidal silver, and knew what it normally cost for that product. $16.67 was an unbelievable price. I'd first heard about colloidal silver two years previously. The friend who told me about it said it cost him $50 for a two-ounce bottle. $16.67 for the Changes product sounded incredibly inexpensive.

But enough about products. I had to ask Scott a tough question. Changes was obviously paying out far more than the average network marketing company. It had been suggested to me that offering to pay out up to 65 percent or 70 percent might eventually prevent the company from sustaining a profit.

"The only thing I can really say to that is we have a lot of experience," Scott responded. "It's my father and myself that started this company. We don't have any outside investors. We used our own personal finances and our life savings to start this. We've already been through the building and rebuilding process with other companies. We have a commitment to our family and our livelihood to make sure this works. I can't stress enough that in designing this we looked at every single angle possible to make sure that this was going to be a lasting thing. It doesn't make any sense for us to go into this halfheartedly. You just wouldn't imagine the amount of work that goes into starting something from scratch. A lot of distributors take for granted becoming a distributor in a company. They're all of a sudden in business for themselves. But going back to day one and coming up with formulations and marketing plans and ordering software and product and brochures and so on—it's an immense amount of work. We don't have any plans of going through all of that work and spending all of our own personal money and have this thing crumble on down the road. I want Changes International to be a 10, 15, 20–year success. I want my children to be able to come in and participate when they grow up. When I have to field those 'Will you be around?' arguments, they normally come from a frustrated distributor."

I didn't say anything. I just listened.

"I can tell you I understand that frustration. Most of the people that come up with these arguments call me without knowing anything about my background or inner workings and they're trying to tell me how much profit I'm not going to make and how my company's not going to last. They're frustrated. And I understand their frustration because I've been there right along with them. They work long and hard in another program and all of a sudden Changes comes along, they get their calculator out, they run the numbers and they say 'Oh, I could be making three or four times as much money.'"

"That's exactly what I hear," I said.

"Yeah, and that's frustrating. I can tell you I wish a program like this would have been available six years ago when I joined my first stairstep breakaway program. I would have been 100 times further ahead of where I am right now. The first stairstep breakaway program I spent three years in, and it took three years of building on a part-time basis. I still held down my full-time job. It took me three years before I was able to walk away from that job. And after all that work, I don't want to name any names because I don't like throwing stones, but finally it achieved a point where I could actually leave my full-time position. My legs got chopped off from underneath me. I got a letter from the company I was working with an attorney general. They said I could no longer practice this particular business in my own backyard. It ended up being time to move on down the road. Really what it boiled down to was who could build a better mousetrap."

I had not achieved the personal success in network marketing that Scott and Terry had enjoyed, but I did understand that a two–level structure, with increments on one side and an "infinity bonus" on the other, rewarded those people who had highly active organizations.

"We are distributors who designed a program for distributors," Scott went on. "As I stated earlier, my father and I have ample business, networking and financing resources backing up this project. One way we cut the fat is that we don't have multiple investors or officers that are sitting at the top of the company being paid large revenues for doing nothing. We don't have right now, and never will have, an elite group of top distributors that year after year earn enormous quarterly and yearly bonuses that end up being paid for by the distributors in the field. We don't right now have big fancy beautiful office suites that most of the distributors in the field would never see but would be paying for."

Scott was truly passionate in stating this. I felt better and better.

"I tell you what we do have, and that is an operation that is so streamlined that two full-time employees can take, process and ship $200,000 worth of product per month. OK? And that's in an area no larger, to put it in perspective, no larger than your living room. Two full-time people can do that. We have streamlined the operation. Our overhead is so low it allows us to be able to pay out much more than other companies, as we discussed earlier. We've got a lot of really excited people, people calling us and saying 'Thank you, thank you, I've been waiting and hoping for something like this for so long. And it's almost too good to be true.'"

I thought, why didn't somebody come up with this structure 20 years earlier? Or maybe they did think of it, and they realized they wouldn't get quite as much profit that way. I'd heard everything I needed to know to get involved. A little more than was necessary to convince me, actually.

Scott wanted to make sure I fully understood everything about the program. He explained to me how they had set up a free information pack system, so that any distributor in Changes International, anywhere in the United States, who had someone even remotely interested in taking a look at the products, would have an information phone line available to all distributors. They only needed to direct the prospect to call.

After they called, a five-page information pack offering complete information on Changes International would be mailed to them. The distributor would follow up with the person a few days later. Interested parties could also receive the information via fax 24 hours a day. All sales aids were produced and sold to the distributor at no profit to the company. This part was of particular interest to me, because I had noticed that many network marketing companies tried to make a profit off their promotional material. My feeling was that such material was a company responsibility, part of the cost of doing business.

"We don't believe in sales aids developing profit for the company," Scott said. "We want to develop sales for the distributor. We have a real nice 'try pack' that the distributor can purchase for 75¢. In most programs, 75¢ would usually buy you nothing, or at most a one–day trial pack. Our company sells a three-day sample for 75¢."

I didn't know of any other network marketing company that would do all this for you. I thought the entire package was incredible and said so.

"Well, we work hard for the distributors in the field," Scott replied. "I appreciate hearing that. And I hear it every day. We have designed something that is achievable and attainable for distributors. Nevertheless, I encourage anybody to do their own homework. Check us out if you like, I always say. Look at the other options available. You'll make the best decision for yourself, and whether it be Changes International or any other company, I just encourage you to at least get involved in network marketing in any way, shape or form. This is an industry to be reckoned with, and I just can't say enough about it."

After one phone call to Scott Paulsen, during which he seemed in no hurry to get on to something else more important, I was hooked. I signed up the next day. I learned a big lesson, talking with Scott.

Namely, you had to take care of the people coming into your company.

The Magic Formula At Last

After talking with Scott, I went over my notes and kept scratching my head over the revolutionary pay plan offered by Changes International. 45 percent on the second level was very significant, because in the two previous years when I had tried to build downlines, with the 5 percent or 6 percent or 10 percent on the second level, it simply did not work. If everything he had told me was true (and I had no reason to doubt him with the amazing distributor retention rate), it dawned on me that the secret ingredient I'd been looking for was a fair pay plan from a company selling good, renewable product.

Ever since then, I've been telling people that the average person has a much better chance of succeeding in network marketing if they have the right pay plan.

Any network marketing pay plan is what it is. It is not a magic formula that only a select few can understand, something you believe in while not comprehending, all the while pushing the products so your dreams come true.

Let me say it again. The average person can succeed in network marketing if they have the right pay plan, as long as they offer good, renewable products and can understand how the pay plan works so that they can easily explain it to others. I could easily understand the Changes pay plan, and had no doubts about my ability to explain it to others. Better yet, Changes had a uniform promotional package that I could get to anyone anywhere, along with a very inexpensive three-day sample.

There was just one problem. I had to contact those people with whom I envisioned building a business. I was pretty darn sure I had the right program at last.

Now I just had to figure out the most effective way for me, the shy guy, to tell as many people about it as possible.

My Own Changes Story

I can't tell you I did not have any doubts at all. I still had lingering doubts from old experiences. If Changes International had not worked out for me, it probably would have been the very last time I ever tried network marketing. Luckily, it was structured so that anyone could understand it, and the products and testimonials (none from celebrities) spoke for themselves. So I tried to analyze everything that had worked for me in previous tries at network marketing, even if the rewards had been only meager.

One thing I knew was that I would have to come up with a way to promote via the mail. I had worked hard to refine this approach in previous programs. Also, I'd had more success than usual with one previous company that had a good audio tape that people liked. (That company's downfall was a breakaway compensation plan. Without bothering to explain it in detail, suffice it to say that as soon as individuals under me reached the top level their checks went down instead of up, so they became discouraged and stopped working, which was frustrating for all of us.)

I never liked to call people. I wanted to do my promotion via the mail because it was much less intrusive. I didn't mind answering phone calls, or talking on the phone as long as they called me first. I simply didn't want to irritate people with a cold call. If they responded, I reasoned, I could mail them copies of the Changes International material Scott had told me about. I might even make up an audio tape and mail that out upon request, if the company didn't have one already prepared. But what could I mail people initially, to get the ball rolling?

I looked back over the Changes International ad that had prompted me to call Scott Paulsen. I reread the sub–headline that had drawn my interest. If it had inspired me, wouldn't it appeal to people of like mind, the kind of folks I could get along with and build a downline? I ran with it. Basically, I took the company's full–page ad and rearranged it a little so that the sub–headline became the headline. Little did I suspect at the time, but that repositioned headline on my one–page flier would become one of the most famous headlines in network marketing history. I didn't create the headline, the company did, but when I elevated it from sub–headline status, people responded in droves:

"NOW YOU CAN MAKE REAL MLM MONEY WITHOUT HAVING A LARGE NUMBER OF DISTRIBUTORS."

I started mailing out this one–page flier, but not to lists purchased from mailing list companies. Remember, I'd worked hard to refine my mailing methods with other programs, and found that blind mailings did not work well. I had no way of verifying whether or not the people on purchased lists were truly interested in new network marketing programs. There was a group of people about whose interests I was sure of though. I knew that anyone who sent me mail, and anyone who advertised in mail order and network marketing publications were actively interested—at least for the moment—in making money in network marketing.

So that's who I mailed to, a list of people I had saved recently and people who listed their addresses in current magazines.

The strategy worked wonders. After mailing out my simple, one–page flier of the redesigned Changes International ad, my phone started ringing. I didn't have to do a bit of selling. Just like Scott Paulsen had done with me, all I did was answer questions and explain the program and the products. I never tried to sell anyone. If they were not interested I simply said OK and good luck.

As more and more people expressed interest and began to sign up, I reminded myself that to be successful I had to actually help those who came into my downline. This was key. I hadn't pursued network marketing as only a business, but as a vehicle to better things. If I had only been interested in making money with no regard for others, I wouldn't have survived. I knew that in any business —

If you truly want to succeed, you have to help others to succeed.

Since I didn't want to spend the rest of my life answering the phones (most people don't), I had to come up with more tools that I could use by mail. My one-page flier soon became two, then four, then six pages. These were all fliers that my downline could reproduce and use as mail-outs. I also designed postcards that my downline could take to their local printer or photocopy shop and have printed.

Still, something was missing. After several years in network marketing I had realized the importance of network marketing pay plans and how most of them simply did not work for normal people. Obviously, I wasn't alone in that experience.

Scott and Terry Paulsen, as proven by their previous successes in network marketing, were good at explaining things to people. I was not an effusive personality, or even as naturally friendly as Scott had been with me on the phone. I had to come up with a way to explain the importance of the Changes International pay plan that would save me repeating the same long story on the phone over and over again.

The Changes I Needed

What I needed was a booklet. I began writing and came up with what is now one of the most photocopied booklets in network marketing history. Rather than selling copies to my distributors for a profit (the mistake that a lot of network marketing companies make), I wanted them to be able to copy it themselves.

I wanted to keep it simple and cheap, and not make the biggest mistake most network marketing companies make in trying to profit from their marketing tools. Why charge your distributors enormous prices for the tools they need to build their business? The easier the access to the tools, the more the distributors will succeed, which makes everyone more money.

The booklet I wrote was called "Secrets of Network Marketing Plans Revealed." It turned out to be an eye–opener for thousands and thousands of network marketers. My telephones rang night and day with people saying how appreciative they were for that booklet. So many had worked so hard at network marketing throughout the years and had not succeeded. They felt like miserable failures. Now, for the first time, they realized that the deck had been stacked against them and they had very little chance of succeeding from the very beginning of most programs. They were so relieved to know that they could finally have success.

After being in Changes for a few months I created an entire system of letters, fliers, postcards, audio tapes and—most importantly—the booklet. This system enabled my downline to work almost entirely by mail. The only time they had to be on the phone was when someone called them to share their excitement or ask questions.

My first check from Changes was $695, my second $1255. The third was $2,710 and they kept on growing from there. Although the company was six months old when I got into it and there were several people making more than $1,000 a month, I soon caught up with them. I became the number one distributor in Changes, and all without ever making recruiting phone calls or giving meetings.

It goes without saying that a shy guy like me would not be someone to give rah–rah recruitment meetings. Personally, I didn't see the sense in them, even if my public presence had been that of a TV talk show host. People get into network marketing for the residual checks, those big checks that they hear about, the ones that come in your mailbox every month, rain or shine. It's easy to get worked up and enthusiastic at a meeting, but you soon realize, even if you have earned some big checks, that with most network marketing programs if you do not keep recruiting like crazy, those checks soon shrivel up to nothing. With most people in most network marketing pay plans you have to keep working or your downline will evaporate very quickly. And so most companies recruit via meetings and personal presentations, which I simply did not want to do.

The Paulsens did not believe in celebrity endorsements. I didn't have TV infomercials to depend upon. They did have tremendous testimonials that stood up against those of anyone. I had to depend on what I could tell people about the company personally.

When promoting any business, you need something you can count on, over and over again. Through good times and bad, by using my easily duplicatable mailing system, my downline was able to keep the ball rolling. After a while, all I really had to do for my existing downline was put out a monthly newsletter. For over two years, I was unavoidably occupied with other pressing issues in my life, yet my checks stayed in a very high range.

The Changes International pay plan simply has never let me down. It just keeps paying and paying. When I look back on what happened to me since joining Changes International, to me it reads like a fairy tale, or someone else's story. I was broke and close to the poverty level all my life, then began earning a stable income that I would not have dreamed possible, at least not for me.

I take my hat off to Scotty and Terry Paulsen, who had the courage to create a network marketing pay plan that enabled the majority of their distributors to succeed and earn a nice part-time income even if they had failed many times before.

To explain more fully how my "shy guy" system worked, let me begin with the booklet that became one of the most reproduced and widely–read marketing tools in network marketing history. I'll go over it in detail in the next chapter.

4
MY SECRETS OF NETWORK MARKETING PLANS REVEALED

After Changes International experienced great success with its pay plan, upwards of 20 companies began emulating it. But that's hindsight. Going in, I didn't know that Changes might be that successful. The truth is, all I could see was that the first two levels of the plan offered big returns. My thought was that the infinity bonus I could take or leave. If I got some returns on that end of the pay plan, great, but I was not about to count on it. Like every "MLM junkie," which is what I was, any time I started with a new company I was always excited. With Changes I had good reason to be enthused, because the 15/45 split was very, very different at the time. Because it was new, though, and therefore I had no other pay plan to compare it to, I truly did not know if it would turn out well for me.

Since I was facing the unknown, potential-wise, I knew that anyone whom I contacted would face the same dilemma, whether they had network marketing experience or not. In fact, I knew I might face a double problem, in that network marketing "conventional wisdom" would say this new company structure could not work. And why not? Because someone would have come up with it before!

It's the same kind of "If God had meant humans to fly he would have given them wings" conventional wisdom that anyone with a truly ground–breaking idea faces. Although I didn't know from my own personal experience that the Changes International plan would work, I was convinced that it could.

How could I convince others? I wasn't a great rah–rah meeting salesperson and didn't plan to start trying to be one. I was resolved to do my convincing via the mail, which was my own ground–breaking idea that most network marketers told me simply would not work. Colds calls were out; I do not call people cold, period. So I started mailing out a one–page flier to anyone who sent me mail. Why not? They were advertising standard network marketing plans and products no better than Changes was selling. If they were piloting Piper Cubs and I had a Lear jet to offer them, wasn't it logical they might fly my way?

That's the same reason I mailed my flier to those who advertised in different mail order and network marketing publications. Ads in magazines aren't cheap. I figured the advertisers were more successful than most network marketers, or they wanted success more than others and were willing to take more of a risk.

In both cases, my reasoning proved out. My phone started ringing a lot. Just as Scott Paulsen had done with me the day I called him, all I did was answer questions and attempted to be helpful. I never tried to sell anyone. If they were not interested after hearing what I had to tell them, I simply wished them good luck and answered the next call. Perhaps I had not been the world's greatest network marketing success with other companies, but I had learned that most people decide whether or not they are interested early on in a conversation. You have a window of opportunity with them, and once they shut that window, you aren't getting in the house.

As mentioned previously, my one-page flier became two pages, then four, then six, all of which my downline could reproduce and mail to potential distributors. The basic essence of the message stayed the same. Let me share with you what that initial one-page flier said. It might give you some idea of why this approach was effective and helped build my business.

The One-Page Flier

"Now you can make REAL MLM money without having to develop a huge network of distributors!!"

* Check by FAX/phone! * Deluxe training packs!
* Free info packs!   * VISA/MASTERCARD

* Extraordinarily high distributor retention rate!

* Earn $450 with 3 active distributors on your 1st level and 9 active distributors on your 2nd!!

* 100% Turnkey for new distributors!!
* Successful, proven 3 step mail order system!

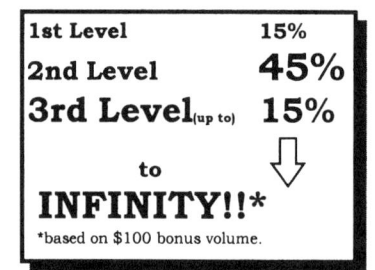

1st Level	15%
2nd Level	**45%**
3rd Level (up to)	15%
to	⇩
INFINITY!!*	
*based on $100 bonus volume.	

CALL NOW!
Before your downline does!!

Fax on Demand
(402)***-****

Free Info Pack
(904)***-****

24hour 2min message
(818)569-3096

Or write:

JOE BROWN

If the flier above appeals to you, you probably see why it worked well for me. I like to think that one reason I had success with my mailings was that I told the truth. I have a lot of faith in people to recognize truth when they see it. I also have a lot of faith in people to be fooled by something that seems like it might be true; that certainly happened with me in other network marketing programs. I was not making a lot of money when the flier just above was first written and mailed out, I also knew that many people starting in network marketing had very limited budgets. So to save them money and increase their ability to mail to as many people as possible, I created a smaller mailer that I thought would be effective.

Postcards Cost Less to Mail Than Fliers

I designed postcards that my downline could take to their local printer or photo copy shop and have printed. They were arranged four to a page on 8.5" x 11" paper, so that anyone in my downline could simply copy the sheet onto card stock, cut it into four pieces, and mail out the cards.

I knew that to be successful I had to continually figure out ways to help those in my downline. This is a key item for anyone in network marketing. If you want to succeed, you have to help others to succeed. To make sure they had tools I knew would work, I shared with them everything I had which I knew people could mail out and get effective responses. One postcard said:

THE HIGHEST PAYING
COMMISSION PROGRAM IN THE HISTORY
OF MULTI-LEVEL!

15% Payout—1st Level
(Black background, larger white letters):
45% PAYOUT—2nd Level
(Normal black letters on white background):
15% potential infinity—3rd Level and Beyond

You no longer need a huge network of Distributors to make Big $ in MLM

Earn $300/month with only 9 Distributors
Earn $1,200/month with only 30 Distributors
Earn $5,000/month with only 120 Distributors

"Changes Int."
Has a Very Low
Distributor Dropout Rate
Most companies have an
85–90%
Distributor Dropout Rate

Products: The 3 top Health Products in the Country
• Join Free by Fax or Phone
• Powerful Short Message—

FREE 24 Hr Information Pack—(phone number)

In creating all my marketing materials I had some great help. I basically came up with headlines and the text of what I wanted to say, then let my friend Pete Harris use his great natural artistic ability to translate my concepts into professionally-presented and highly effective marketing materials.

You do *not* have to go to professional advertising agencies for your "collateral materials." You can usually find someone with fantastic creative abilities in your local college, or by placing a simple ad in a newspaper. If you're a computer dunce like me and aren't able to create flyers and postcards and such things on your own, I suggest you find someone to help you.

Later, when I developed the two-minute phone message with which I open this book, we created another postcard:

The Most Effective Ad & Postcard

THIS WAS MY MOST EFFECTIVE AD EVER!

I used this ad as a full-page ad, a quarter-page ad, and as a postcard. People really identified with "a ten-time loser" because so many network marketers have tried many times and failed. So when they saw that someone who had lost many times could succeed, it gave them hope that they could succeed also.

Later, after I interviewed Scott Paulsen about Changes International and made a tape of that conversation available to Changes distributors, I offered another postcard. This time I added a few graphics and some different fonts, but again it was all black and white and nothing very fancy.

TEN TIMES LOSER
FINDS THE RIGHT ONE!

TEN TIME LOSER
finds the right one...

0 - $10,000
in 6 months!!!

None of these ads or postcards were in any way elaborate. They just told the truth.

There's another postcard I used, but not until I developed the mailing item that really made my business take off and helped my downline tremendously. Despite the success we were having, I felt something was missing. It wasn't something I would find, though, it was something I would create, a simple mailer that put me over the top. After it proved to be a smash success, I made the postcard version of my first ad, copied "four–up" (four ads on one sheet that you can cut into sections and mail as postcards):

FIND OUT!!

How I Earned $100,000 Part-Time in Network Marketing in 1995!
All by Mail!

1. Without ever giving or attending a single meeting.

2. Without ever calling anyone on the phone unless they called me first.

Get the most photocopied booklet of 1995 "Secrets of Network Marketing Revealed." Just fill in your name and address below!

Name_____

Address_____

City, State, Zip_____

FAX me or return this card to:
JOE BROWN

This ad was my second most effective ever. I used the text of this ad both as a magazine ad (full page & quarter page) and as a postcard.

After several years in network marketing I had realized the importance of network marketing pay plans and how the average plan simply did not work for most people. Even though my distributors and I were having success sending out mailings and talking to people who called, I knew that wasn't good enough for the kind of expansion and profits we wanted. I had to come up with a way to explain the importance of the Changes International pay plan. What I needed was a booklet. I began writing and came up with what is now one of the most photocopied booklets in network marketing history. I wanted my distributors to be able to copy it themselves. As you might have guessed from reading the postcards above, all I wanted for my efforts was my cost of producing these promotional materials.

Let me repeat an important point:

ONE OF THE BIGGEST MISTAKES
NETWORK MARKETING COMPANIES
MAKE IS TRYING TO EARN A PROFIT
FROM THEIR MARKETING TOOLS.

In my opinion, such an approach is really dumb. Why charge your distributors enormous prices for the tools they need to build their business? The easier the access to the tools, the more the distributors will succeed, which makes everyone more money.

The booklet I wrote was called "Secrets of Network Marketing Plans Revealed." It was an eye-opener for thousands and thousands of network marketers. I don't mean to brag, but this thing worked better than any marketing tool I had ever seen. My telephones rang night and day with people telling how appreciative they were for that booklet. So many had worked so hard at network marketing throughout the years and had not succeeded, they felt like miserable failures.

Now, for the first time, they realized that the deck had been stacked against them and they had very little chance of succeeding from the very beginning, with other programs. They were extremely relieved and buoyantly happy to know that they could finally have success.

After only a few months in Changes, I had created an entire system of letters, fliers, postcards, audio tapes and, most importantly, the booklet.

Before I knew it, I had developed a system which enabled my downline to work almost entirely by mail. The only time they had to be on the phone was when someone called them to share their excitement or ask a few questions.

As I said earlier, my opinion is that people get into network marketing for that big residual check that keeps arriving in your mailbox every month, rain or shine. With the promotional materials I developed, we had a fully operational turnkey system that worked very well. It was completely duplicatable. When I hit a period when I was not able to work and could only write a monthly newsletter, the Changes pay plan simply would not let me down and kept paying and paying.

Don't get me wrong. We never downplayed the high quality Changes International products. There was no reason to do so. We had testimonials that would stand up against those of any other network marketing company, like the one I mentioned earlier where one distributor went on "The Maury Povich Show" to talk about her absolutely amazing weight loss of over 200 pounds. Now our products are even better thanks to

Twin Labs who was recently voted nutritional manufacturer of the year.

I had been broke and close to the poverty level all my life, then learned to make a stable income that I had previously only dreamed was possible. It was my feeling that the majority of existing and potential distributors out there would be most interested in hearing about a network marketing pay plan that enabled distributors to succeed and earn a nice part-time income, because many of them had—like me—failed many times before. Instead of a package of information, I wanted to explain the essence of our opportunity in one complete package, something anyone could read through easily in one sitting. I needed a booklet.

When I sat down to write the booklet, I thought of the continual search I had been on for years, and how I had been convinced there were secrets to network marketing success that I simply had not been able to find. I also knew that Changes International, with its revolutionary pay plan, was a company that had changed the history of network marketing forever. This gave me the title of my booklet and the subheadline on the cover:

SECRETS
of Network Marketing Plans
Revealed

Do not join any MLM program
until you read this booklet!

The booklet evolved, as does any publication that goes through multiple printings. What I present to you here is the 4th edition which was sent to my downline. Again, please remember that all these sheets were created with a normal word processing program and printed onto regular 8.5" x 11" sheets of paper, so that all the distributor needed to do was reproduce the sheets and staple them in the middle before mailing them out.

If you're trying to tell someone about something truly innovative, you're handicapped in that they have nothing to compare it to. You can, however, tell them the essential points of what's wrong with things they know about which are in the same arena. And if that explanation is news, all the better. Most network marketers I knew didn't realize that many network marketing companies wanted and expected new distributors to fail and drop out. They didn't realize that by initially buying a large amount of product from a network marketing company to get started was the way most of those companies made their money. Well, I didn't hesitate to tell them because I had something that *would* work! Here is the text of the booklet.

❖   ❖   ❖

SECRETS OF NETWORK MARKETING PLANS REVEALED
by Joe Brown

Network Marketing is truly one of the original Golden Opportunities of our time. No vehicle other than the lottery can enable an individual without formal training to earn such vast sums of money.

There are multiple thousands of people today who earn a six figure or more annual income through Network Marketing. Many of these people don't even have high school diplomas.

It is possible for you to also make an annual income on par with and above many company executives or degreed professionals. But in order to do this there are a few things you must understand first.

The Facts You May Not Want to Hear... But Need To Know

As wonderful as MLM is, the hard truth is that most people who get involved fail.

In fact, the statistics prove year after year that 90 percent of the individuals who get into Network Marketing never see a check for more than $200 the entire time they are in and most lose money.

WHY DO SO MANY FAIL?

There are two reasons why most people never make a cent in Network Marketing. The first is known and usually stated as the one and only reason people fail. If you have not yet guessed, it is... PEOPLE DO NOT WANT TO SELL!

Most of us do not like trying to corner someone and talk them into buying a product or a service. If they say no, we take it personally and human beings do not like rejection.

But there is another major reason why people fail at Network Marketing that is not generally recognized.

These plans are cleverly and deceptively structured so that the company makes money and a few so-called Heavy Hitters make money, so the little guy and gal loses out.

They make these plans so difficult that even a natural born salesperson will not make the grade if they are working with a bad marketing plan.

Case in point. I recently returned from a seminar where several highly gifted and personable people were describing to those of us in the audience how they had worked at several other MLM companies previously, recruited hundreds and hundreds of people and their monthly checks were miserably small in comparison to the amount of effort they put in.

If people of this caliber can't make the grade with a tricky marketing plan, how can the rest of us average people do it? The correct answer is WE CAN NOT.

Yet when they got into a company that had a more fair and distributor focused marketing plan many ended up making sums of money in the six figure range.

This is the kind of money highly paid professionals with years of experience make and these people did it in less than two years with a fair compensation plan and good products.

What we can do is educate ourselves about Network Marketing plans so that we are not snared in by the hype, celebrity endorsements, or other promotions Network Marketing companies use today.

The pay plans for MLM companies in the past have come under three categories:

First is the break away. These plans have large qualifications you have to attain before you can start making any serious money. And then there are additional qualifications you have to maintain once you are at the top in order to continue to receive the bonus money.

The simple fact is that only very experienced MLMers or those who really have the gift of gab ever make these qualifications, or people buy the position and have a garage full of products they can't sell. Many of you have learned this the hard way.

The second type of pay plan is the Force Matrix. These plans promise spill over which hardly ever comes to pass, plus you have to have a gazillion people before you start making any real money. Most people loose at this one also, although on the surface it's very attractive because it seems to guarantee upline help.

The third type of plan is the Binary. Here you have to keep two groups of people perfectly balanced in group volume.

This is much, much more difficult than you would possibly imagine, plus it takes hours on the phone talking with your people, finding out their personal volume and keeping them stacked just to enable you to profit.

Another reason many marketing plans do not work is because of the payout on various levels. Although there is some variety to this, most plans are structured like this:

1st Level	5-10%	2nd Level	5-10%
3rd Level	5-10%	4th Level	5-10%
5th Level	5-10%	6th Level	5-10%

In actuality, any particular level can vary from as low as 1 percent to a high of 15 percent. But if any particular level has this high of 15 percent you can be sure all the remaining levels pay 5 percent or less.

So you have to get people way down on the sixth level or lower to get the 50-60 percent potential that most companies brag about. This simply takes too long before you get into profit.

Not only does this take more time than the average distributor is financially ready to handle, but they also have to deal with the fact that the new distributors they have managed to recruit start falling by the wayside almost from the beginning. So it is a continual treadmill of catch up to replace these short-lived distributors. This quickly becomes very discouraging.

Another discouraging aspects of MLM's are the payout plans.

Most marketing plans have an average potential payout of 50 to 60 percent of your monthly purchase. But the key word here is potential.

The truth is that this potential is only realized by the few Heavy Hitters at the top of the company. The majority of distributors never come close to that.

In fact, the average payout of the Network Marketing industry in general is a measly 25-30 percent. Only half of what they claim the potential is.

Where does the other 30 percent of the money go? Right back into the companies pockets. So where most assume that any particular MLM company is working on a 40 percent profit margin, they are in fact working with more like a 70 percent PROFIT MARGIN.

Is it any wonder that hundreds of MLM companies spring up every year?! As soon as someone realizes these numbers, they go out and start their own company. And as long as they last, they make a bundle thanks to the average distributor who is in fact financing this operation for them.

THE MOST REVOLUTIONARY & INGENIOUS MARKETING PLAN EVER DEVELOPED!

I know this is a bold statement, but we have HARD FACTS & STATISTICS to back this up.

Now, there is a new and different type of pay plan that not only conquers all these previously mentioned obstacles, but also enables a new distributor to quickly get in profit and thus stay in the program longer. The obvious result is EVERYBODY PROFITS!

Those of you who are new to Network Marketing may not have the experience or knowledge to grasp the significance of the ASTOUNDING numbers we are about to give you.

But keep on reading and if you know someone who has been in the business for a few years, they will verify these FACTS. And we repeat...

FACTS THAT ARE ABSOLUTELY PHENOMENAL.

As we mentioned at the beginning, the annual retention rate for most MLMs today is about 10 percent. Some do a little better and some do a lot worse. I have seen companies brag in gigantic headlines of a 25-35 percent retention rate and one or two claims a 50 percent annual distributor retention rate.

The marketing plan I will describe to you has a CPA-audited, 2-year, 75 percent retention rate that's the highest in the industry! Our numbers totally obliterate all records or claims that any other MLM has ever had. Why are so many staying active?

BECAUSE WE ARE MAKING MONEY!

This NEW compensation plan has a potential payout of 75 percent and an average ACTUAL PAYOUT of 60 percent! This is 80 percent of the potential as compared with the industry average of 50 percent of the potential and this 60 percent actual payout is 200 percent the industry average.

Totally unlike the payout of the other compensation plans we reviewed that have payout plans of a measly 5-10 percent per level, THIS COMPENSATION PLAN PAYS...

1st Level   15%!
2nd Level   45%!!
3rd Level   up to 15% Infinity Bonus!!!
*$100 bonus volume

Finally, after 50 years of Network Marketing, someone came up with a plan where the average distributor can get in and instead of having a 10 percent chance of making money, he or she has a 90 percent plus chance.

All it takes is 3 active people on your first level who each enroll 3 active people on your second level and you can earn $450 per month!!

Now let's briefly go back to the other reason most people fail in MLM... MOST PEOPLE DO NOT AND CAN NOT SELL.

GOOD NEWS!
THIS PROBLEM HAS BEEN SOLVED!

Thanks to the modern technology of audio tapes, you can succeed in Network Marketing and never have to approach friends, relatives (or anyone within three feet as most companies try and get you to do) or anyone for that matter.

Using this cassette and mail-order system, it is possible to become successful in Network Marketing without:

1. Giving or attending a single meeting.

2. Approaching strangers. (In fact, most of my friends and associates don't have the slightest idea that I do Network Marketing as a side business.)

3. Without ever calling one single person on the phone unless they called me first and specifically

asked me to return their call. And then, I only answered questions.

How is this possible? I have developed a system of ready made and very POWERFUL ads and postcards that you get when you join my downline. These ads and cards bring loads of individuals who are looking for the perfect opportunity we have for them.

Then we send them a FACT FILLED and VERY CONVINCING audio tape that virtually closes the sale. As a member of my downline you can purchase an unlimited quantity for 55 cents each. (That's about 50 percent of what it could cost you to do them yourself.)

When a prospect calls, they do not need any additional selling. They probably just want to express their enthusiasm, ask how quickly they can get going and maybe ask a few simple questions. If you cannot answer them, your sponsor, myself, or the company will answer them. It is as simple as that.

A 100 PERCENT TURNKEY SYSTEM
THAT ENABLES A NEW OR INEXPERIENCED
DISTRIBUTOR TO GET STARTED IMMEDIATELY!

Here's how it works:

1. New distributor purchases a 6 pack of product from the company. These are time tested products that work... Thermo-Lift, Multi-Zyme, Perfor-Max, Colloidal Silver, 4-in-1, and Colloidal Minerals. Buy any combination you like.

2. New distributor obtains our 3 step mail order system from their sponsor, or purchases this from Joe Brown for $10. This package includes: 1. sample of the first mailing, 2. sample of the second mailing, 3. the Artwork package of computer originals from which the distributor can make their own first and second step (after adding their own

name, address and phone on each flyer). This is shipped 2day Priority Mail.

3. Distributor mails out first step with coupon to MLM prospects. I have had very little luck with MLM lists but have had much better results by mailing counter-offers to those who send me MLM offers in the mail and by mailing to those who run display ads in MLM or mail order publications. People who send you mail or advertise are MLM Workers—this is what we want. Not lookie-loos or new people. A list of MLM publications is included in the artwork package.

4. When prospects return coupon with money or stamps, they are sent the second step which includes an audio tape, booklet, application and more information. Most of the tapes can be purchased from Joe Brown for only 55 cents a piece plus a small shipping charge. (Described elsewhere.)

5. When prospects receive the second step they are 95 percent sold. They will call distributor prospects and ask a few simple questions and they are ready to get in. If the new person has had some success they are placed on the 1st level. If they have had little success, they are placed on the 2nd. A new distributor is placed on your second level by having them write in the name and ID# of someone on your 1st level in the optional ID line.

6. Tell the new distributor about the three step system and they are ready to repeat the process.

7. You now have a new distributor sponsored into the fastest paying and highest paying MLM in existence today, complete with a proven three step mail order system.

THE COMPANY THAT WORKS FOR YOU...

THE MARKETING PLAN THAT WORKS FOR YOU...

THE 3-STEP ALL-BY MAIL SYSTEM THAT WORKS FOR YOU!!

❖ ❖ ❖

Comparison Page

That was the bulk of the booklet, which laid out a simple explanation of the Changes International plan. In the middle of the booklet were two pages: (a) Distributor Application & Agreement (with Terms and Conditions on the reverse); and (b) Order Form. Both of these pages came directly from the company, and were self–explanatory. All anyone sending out the booklet needed do was fill in their own name and ID number (Social Security or Federal ID) in the Sponsor Information box of the Distributor Application & Agreement. It couldn't have been more simple.

To reinforce the idea of how Changes was better than any other similar plan out there, I next included information about other companies.

There's Just No Comparison...

Let's take a look at **CHANGES INTERNATIONAL**. We provide excellent products, support and a means to make outstanding profits! Let's say you enroll 3 people and they each enroll 3 people (that's 9 people on your second level, a total of 12 people). Everyone is doing $100 worth of product every month. Here's how much commission you would be paid by other companies, as compared to **CHANGES:**

Company A 1st level is 5% and the 2nd level is 5%	$60
Company B 1st level is 5% and the 2nd level is 5%	$60
Company C 1st level is 8% and the 2nd level is 8%	$96
Company D 1st level is 8% and the 2nd level is 10%	$114
Company E 1st level is 30% bonus and the 2nd level is 5%	$135

But with **CHANGES INTERNATIONAL** you can make **$450***
1st level is 15% and the 2nd level is 45%

No sign up fees, plus earn 40-45% retail profit, plus the opportunity to earn up to 15% 3rd level-to-Infinity Bonus!!

*these samples are not promises of income but simply represent your potential.

Reinforcement Page
The last page of the booklet reinforced the positive benefits of being a part of Changes International, and listed the five products offered by the company at the time with a short descriptive paragraph of each.

Inside Back Cover & Back Cover
As mentioned, the booklet covered herein was the 4th edition. I used yellow paper for covers. Some of my distributors used other colors they thought were more attractive to the eye. So, since the covers were copied separately on colored paper, we could change various announcements and new developments made by the company. I placed these on the inside back cover, while on the back cover I repeated the inside front cover "Did You Know?" message with my phone number and the sentence "Hear an unusual 2 minute message." There was also a box that said "FACTS THAT OTHER NETWORK MARKETING COMPANIES DON'T WANT YOU TO KNOW!!" and another box that encouraged distributors to send the booklet via First Class Mail so recipients would take the mailing more seriously.

Lastly, there was a place for the recipient to fill in their name and address. They would return that page with $3 or 10 stamps to receive more information about Changes International and my three-step system.

Why This Booklet Worked
Although I've laid out the booklet that became famous here, describing what went into putting it together, I didn't tell you this:

It had typos, even with the 4th edition. No one complained.

It was not written by a professional copywriter, or laid out by a graphics artist.

I wrote the text of the booklet and Pete Harris designed and formatted it with a simple desktop publishing program, using the fonts and emphases that I thought appropriate. My criterion was simply that it looked good to me.

Last but not least, it was not written for rocket scientists. I've been told that the average reading level of most Americans is fifth grade. I knew that many people who get into network marketing do not have advanced college degrees, but then again many did. I didn't think about any of that. I simply wrote what I had to say in simple terms that I thought anyone could easily understand.

Plus, I told the truth, and that works. A famous comedian who started his own network marketing company, said that "Truth is the baby of the world. It never gets old." Maybe people had never seen a pay plan like Changes, but many of the people I recruited had experience with other network marketing companies. They knew what lies were. I figured that by telling them the truth, I could trust them to see the possibilities, just as I had.

With my two-minute phone message, my taped interview with Scott Paulsen, and the booklet I've detailed here, I was able to provide folks in my downline with a package of materials that allowed them to get out of the way and let the selling be done for them.

Nevertheless, everyone is different. No matter how good the basic materials you provide are, everyone has to create their own system that works best for them. As my downline grew and the promotional materials and methods changed and were shared, I began putting out a monthly letter to keep everyone up to date, and I was often surprised at what we all learned.

5
PROFESSIONAL SALES = NETWORK MARKETING SUCCESS

It didn't take long for the booklet I created to become the #1 selling tool for myself and my downline. I believe it was so effective because it explained the Changes International pay plan in simple terms. If you surveyed 100 percent of all distributors of all network marketing companies today, you might find that less than 10 percent of those network marketers truly understand the pay plan under which they are working. That's my estimation, anyway. Personally, I wonder sometimes if my frustration about ever achieving the upper levels of pay plans in other companies had something to do with the fact that I did not fully understand those plans.

It's easy to get enthusiastic about a program when you fully understand it and believe in the company and its products. Nothing motivates people like genuine enthusiasm.

They also tend to get enthusiastic when they realize they don't have to be geniuses to use a program and make a great part-time income.

As I said, my booklet was not written by a professional copywriter, or laid out by a graphics artist. It was written by me and designed by Pete Harris. I didn't set out to do something that looked homemade. I just had to use what I had available.

Mark Twain said that some writers' books were like fine wines, while his were like water, and that a lot more people drank water. My booklet was water. It explained network marketing pay plans to the average person.

As simple as it was, though, not just anyone could have written it. Decades of experience of Scott and Terry Paulsen went into their design of the Changes International structure, and I had years of experience behind me. So a lot of education went into that little booklet, even if some of the learning came from the School of Failed Pay Plans.

That's why, if you find yourself floundering in trying to get a network marketing program going, you should rely on professionals to help you do your selling. You need to read as much as you can, stay in touch with people who brought you into the program, and watch what other programs are doing right and doing wrong. You may find audio and video tapes which help you make your case in recruiting distributors, and I'm sure you'll get help from any company you join, but I advise you not to load up with too many such tools. The old KISS rule (Keep It Simple, Stupid) works pretty well. You don't want to confuse or overwhelm people with material.

My Three-Step System

My other key tool was the two–minute message tape I made, the one you read at the beginning of the book. That little two-minute voice message was one of the best things I ever did. Distributors all around the world use it. Last time I checked it was being used in London, England and Sydney, Australia, even Germany. Again, I just stated my case succinctly and my enthusiasm was real. My downline didn't have to worry about creating their own voice message. They mailed out printed material and had people listen an average guy describe the essence of the Changes program. This tape helped me go from zero distributors to 5,000 in only four months!

Watch Who You Work With

Here's a professional secret, a subtle thing that might help you qualify prospects. Any good salesperson knows that you can work yourself to death dealing with lookie–loos who have no intention of joining your program. You know the type—professional "samplers" who never buy anything but will take all the free samples you'll give out, like the elderly man in Michigan I heard about. He was kind of broke, barely had enough money to keep his place warm in the winter. He wrote off for junk mail, once he realized he could get it for free. He pursued every free offer he could possibly get in the mail, and he tied up all the paper into bundles and put them in his fireplace and kept himself warm that winter. I'm sure some of those pages came from network marketing companies he called on 800 numbers! I can't blame him for using his ingenuity to stay cozy, but I don't like the idea of my efforts and hard–won cash going up in smoke!

We listed the company's 800 number on our mailings, but after someone called and listened to my two-minute message, they then had to place a toll call to find out more information. They had to pay to play, so to speak. Because I was in the tape business, I had a kind of an advantage in that I could buy tapes pretty inexpensively and get them duplicated for very little. Once I made the tape, I did not try to make a profit on it. Rather than try to make money off it, I transferred the savings to my downline, so that they could get the tapes almost as cheap as I could. Similarly, when I sat down to write the booklet, I didn't think "I'm going to write a booklet that's going to make me a lot of money." What I thought was "Now I understand pay plans and I understand why this is better. If I'm going to be successful, I need to put this in a format that my downline can understand." The idea of the booklet wasn't to make me rich; the idea was to help my downline understand.

As effective as these two tools were, we still needed something else that explained more background on the company. Changes International offers very nice color brochures and booklets which explain the company and its products, including two pages of Frequently Asked Questions (FAQs), but I discovered that people asked me over and over about how the company started and what the founders of the company were all about.

If you use a computer and look for information about a software package on a Website (www.quicken.com for example) you're used to the idea of FAQs. I didn't have a Website on which to post my FAQs. Although I never minded talking on the phone with potential distributors or those already in my downline, I did grow weary of repeatedly answering the same sort of questions about the beginnings and philosophy of Changes International. So I got a professional to do my selling. I called Scott Paulsen and interviewed him on the phone, taping our conversation. This became a two-sided tape entitled "CHANGES

INTERNATIONAL and Message from the President." It was a simple audio tape, nothing fancy, no special artwork or case. People loved it—it filled a need.

I charged $3 for the whole package of my booklet, my two-minute message, and the two-sided taped conversation with Scott Paulsen. The booklet was mailed as flat 8.5 x 11 pages that could be taken to the printer or photocopy shop and made up by each distributor. I sold individual audio tapes—"Facts That Network Marketing Companies Don't Want You To Know" (with Side Two being "The Most Powerful Downline Building and Training System Ever Developed") and the Changes Testimonial Tape—to my downline for 55¢ each. That's about as cheap as it gets, and believe me, my distributors appreciated the gesture.

I ended up charging $10 for the whole system because I wanted a little bit of a qualification, just like I'd make people pay for a toll call (unless they lived in the same area as me) after they'd made the initial call to the 800 number. Otherwise, I figured, I'd have every Tom, Dick and Harry in the whole world wanting a look at this thing. As it was, the items in the three-part package cost me just a little less than $10 (including postage) to produce. If someone couldn't afford $10, I reasoned, they couldn't afford the small amount of money to buy enough product from Changes to get started.

When I ran ads I always said "Send me $3 or 10 first class stamps for a tape or other information." I wanted to qualify those respondents, too.

Anyone who joined my downline received my Three-Step System, which is as follows:

1. They mailed the booklet "Secrets of Network Marketing Plans Revealed" out to people who sent

them offers in the mail, people who advertised in network marketing or mail order publications, people who answered their ads, or people whose names and addresses they purchased from a list company (I advised them on where to find decent lists, although I didn't encourage buying such lists).

2. When prospects returned the last page of the booklet with their name and address filled out, and $3 or 10 U.S. postage stamps, my distributor would send the prospect some Changes material including written testimonials and one or both of the Changes audio tapes. Before we had the booklet in its current form, this step included sending the prospect the company application and product order form, and the pay plan as well (now those items are included in the booklet).

3. When the prospect signed up, my distributor would tell the prospect they could purchase the complete artwork package (which meant they could make up their own booklets) and audio tape from me for $10. Once these items were ordered, they were always sent 2-3 day priority mail. I listed my name and address and fax number, so that if someone wanted to fax me their credit card number they could expedite the process.

This system did not have to take long to get someone started, and it worked very well. A $10 investment to get the basic promotional material to start your own lucrative part-time business is a pretty reasonable deal, wouldn't you say?

The 100% "Plug In and Play" Turnkey System

My approach to building and maintaining a successful downline has always been to do as much as possible to give my distributors good tools that they can simply put to work without having to think much about it. I wanted to keep it simple all down the line, so I put together a "plug in and play" 100 percent turnkey system which anyone in our company could use. Here's how it works:

1. The new distributor purchases a six-pack of product from the company. All these are time-tested products that work such as: *Thermo-Lift, Perfor-Max, Colloidal Silver, Four-in-One, Colloidal Minerals* and *Multi-Zyme*. (We have more than 20 products at the time of this writing and are continually adding more.) New distributors can buy any combination they like. (Note: Though the products may change, we always encourage distributors to have at least a sample of all the basic products the company offers. This does not mean that we ever attempt to overload new distributors with huge inventory purchases, like other companies do. That would probably be a sure sign that the company is not interested in long-term association with distributors.)

2. The new distributor obtains the three-step mail order system from their sponsor (as outlined above), or purchases it from me for $10. This package includes: (a) sample of the first mailing, (b) sample of the second mailing, (c) the artwork package of computer originals from which the distributor can make their own first and second step (after adding their own contact information). This system is shipped two-day Priority Mail.

3. The distributor mails out the first step (the booklet) to network marketing prospects. I always stress to them that I've had very little luck with network marketing lists and that I've had much better results by mailing counter-offers to those who send me network marketing offers in the mail or to those who run display ads in network marketing or mail order publications. People who send out network

marketing mail or advertise are workers. That is precisely the public you want to reach, not lookie-loos or people brand-new to network marketing. A list of network marketing publications is included in the artwork package they received in step (2)(a) above.

4. When prospects return the coupon from the booklet listing their name and address, along with the amount of money or stamps requested, they are sent the second step, which includes an audio tape, booklet, application and more information. Additional tapes can be purchased for only 55¢ each plus a small shipping charge.

5. I've found that when prospects receive the second step they are 95 percent sold. They will call distributors and ask a few simple questions and unless someone says something that really puts them off, they are ready to get involved. If the new person has had some previous success in network marketing, they are placed on the first level. If they have had little success, they are placed on the second level—all purchasing $100 of product per month—so they can be nurtured by people on the first level. New distributors are placed on the second level of the person who sent them the booklet; they simply write in the name and ID number of a person on the recruiting distributor's first level in the "optional ID" line.

6. The new distributor is then told about the three-step system and they are ready to repeat the process.

7. The new distributor has now been sponsored into the fastest paying and highest paying network marketing company in existence, complete with a proven three-step mail order system.

Personally, I think the above is the most complete, easily repeatable success system ever developed. A grammar school student could do it! All it takes is three active people on someone's first level who each enroll three active people on their second level and the initial distributor can earn $450 per month, with a company that has the high retention rate and the most attainable pay-out in network marketing today.

When I shared the above ideas with people I asked them to not be blindly loyal to their present program, particularly if they were not making good money. When you add up the figures, you make $30 to $40 per every active distributor in your downline, per month. It wasn't hard to convince them, because they could easily compare my claims to what they currently had going. Here's a letter I sent out to established network marketers:

❖ ❖ ❖

Dear Network Marketing Professional,

The purpose of this letter is NOT to talk you out of your program and get you into mine. Rather, it's to help you salvage some of those leads you worked so hard to obtain that did not pan out.

For whatever reason, your prospect found or thought they found something in your opportunity that did not appeal to them. Once you have given your best, there it not much you can do, you might think.

Think again.

Why not offer them another opportunity (because you know they are looking) that is completely different? It is working splendidly for me. I am getting a high response rate from those who turned down my first program.

If you are an experienced Network Marketer I think you will see from the enclosed flier that this company has conquered right up front many of the "objections" you and I are so tired of hearing.

I have never seen a program that enables someone to "get into profit" so quickly. Three people and you are home free, with a whopping 60 percent payout from your first two levels. They even mail out company literature for you for FREE!

Please don't throw this out because of misdirected loyalty to your present company. Once again, please continue to make your present company your number one effort.

But letting all those unclosed leads go to waste is not helping your company or your own bank account.

Give it some thought. Then call me if you have questions.

Sincerely,

P.S. If after reading this, you still don't plan to use those leads, I might consider purchasing them from you.

❖   ❖   ❖

Not a bad letter if I do say so myself. How could anyone turn it down? I told them to stay with their present company, and I offered to buy their leads from them, even if they weren't interested in my program. How many letters like that have you ever received in the mail? (Letters from me or my distributors don't count, of course.)

Admit It When You're Stealing

After NFL quarterback Joe Namath led the amazing New York Jets to an amazing underdog Superbowl victory in 1969, he became a national figure, appearing in movies, TV shows and commercials long after his football career was cut short by injuries. The slogan of one of those commercials was "If you've got it, flaunt it." Though I encouraged people to stay in their own programs while investigating what I could offer them with Changes International, I never hesitated to tell them that I often signed up distributors from other network marketing companies. Why not? It was going on all the time, and with good reason—I had the pay plan that made the most sense, and I flaunted it. In my opinion, you should never hesitate go after good distributors from another company, if you truly think you're doing them a favor by getting them involved with your own program. That's part of the network marketing world, and in case you haven't noticed lately, that's how international corporate recruiters work as well. If you have a better program, by getting successful network marketers on board, you're doing both of you a favor. Toward that end, here's one flier I mailed out:

I'm a Thief! I admit it!

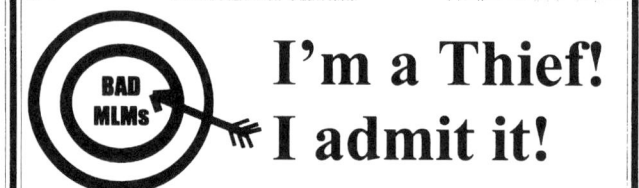

I steal distributors from other big MLM companies and heavy hitters. At least, that's what they say.

How do I do this? Easy. I simply show them my company's marketing plan and prove to them with copies of my checks that I constantly earn

$30 per distributor!

Then when they look at their print out and see they're earning between $5 and $10 per distributor (if that), they ask, "How do I get in?"

I steal from the rich and give to the poor. (Formerly poor, that is.) I'm getting to be known as the Robin Hood of MLM.

If you are tired of being the beaten down and broke servant of the Sheriff of Nottingham, come join my merry band of prosperous distributors.

Send this ad and $3 or 10 first class stamps for complete information and an amazing audio tape to:
JOE BROWN

24hour 2min message (818)569-3096

Promote Network Marketing As A Viable Idea

For people new to network marketing or for those having little experience, it is important to engender the idea of the more affluent and even healthy lifestyle that can result from being a network marketer. Any time I saw an article that I thought would help create enthusiasm for network marketing, I would tell my distributors about it. If I liked the article enough, I share it with my downline. One of my favorites was in the December 1995 issue of *Success* magazine. It gave specific examples of how dentists, real estate salespersons, doctors, attorneys, engineers, even politicians were making great money with network marketing programs. The doctor mentioned in the article, a surgeon in Detroit, Michigan, was making $1.3 million a year from his clinic and practice, but he and his wife were making approximately 75 percent of that amount part–time in network marketing!

Granted, they were top–level distributors in their company and had been at it a while, but an article about real people in top professions with this kind of income potential is enough to legitimize network marketing to anyone but the most cynical (who you don't want in your organization, anyway).

Don't be afraid to say how well you're doing in network marketing, if you are, and why you are able to steal people from other programs or even other professions. If you can back up your claims, you're not bragging. You're merely stating the facts, and no one can argue with that.

Let Other People Do Your Convincing

As you know, I'm no fan of celebrity endorsements, because I think they are relatively useless in network marketing. I do believe, however, in product testimonials from normal people, when it comes to touting the benefits of company products. There may be laws against using such testimonials in your given area (it has to do with making medical claims), so you have to check with an attorney or company headquarters before mailing out testimonials.

It goes back to the same problem I had before—I'm just not a good "pitchman" in person, and I've found that not many people are. While building my business, I would sometimes include product testimonials in my mailings to share how others were enjoying the products. Often that was enough to convince someone to try a product, particularly if the testimonial came from someone they could look up in the phonebook. (Generally, most people don't want the bother of calls from the public, and so are only willing to have their initials listed, but on occasion some folks feel so strongly about the products they don't mind who asks.)

I could list dozens of product testimonials in this book, but I do not feel that they are key to what I am trying to share with you, which is how to build your own network marketing business. For that reason, I will leave how you choose to deal with testimonials up to you and the company you represent. I urge you, however, to check with your company to determine what their policy on the use of testimonials may be. Additionally, you may want to get a legal opinion before publishing testimonials. Also, make certain that you get the OK to publish any testimonials your distributors share, even if you are only using their initials. Get the permission in writing.

Real statements from real people about real results do more to sell any product or company than anything else out there. We may live in a media–intensive, public relations world, but people are much more likely to trust something a friend tells them than anything else. The next best thing to word of mouth is written testimonials.

Stealth Recruiting

Before you think you have my methods totally figured out, here's another aspect of my "quiet guy" approach that I haven't mentioned. Another thing I do to recruit distributors is leave behind postcards—which are actually little ads—and audio tapes in public places for people to discover. I recruited my #1 distributor by leaving a tape at a public place near my home. People might throw away paper postcards, but they're much more reluctant to throw away an audio tape. Even those I sold for 55¢ each to my downline are a small cost to recruit the top person in your organization!

My distributor found the tape on the chair, put it in her purse, and listened to it later. When she was done, she called me and she asked me some questions, which I answered, and she said "Well, let me think about it." She didn't think long before deciding to sign up, and she became my #1 distributor, eventually making $20,000 a month.

My tape was the most valuable thing she ever found! Of course, it's also the most valuable tape I ever abandoned, so we both got lucky that day.

On the other hand, you have to know where you can leave stuff laying around and where you can't. If you leave a tape somewhere in a mall, for example, you'll probably get zero results. I've watched this; I experimented. Kids hang out in malls, and that's who will pick up a tape there. If you're going to spend money for a tape and leave it around for someone to find, you have to make sure that it's somewhere where adults will notice it. I would go to the mall and I'd put tapes on benches and by escalators, and I'd stand to the side and I'd watch. Kids, kids, kids. Parents would go by and not look twice, while kids would pick the tape up. So you have to put a tape somewhere where an adult will discover it, not a kid. Similarly, it generally takes an adult to pick up a postcard, which kids could care less about.

I don't plant tapes extensively. I never got in my car and drove around with the express purpose of leaving tapes or postcards in any given location, but I do keep some in my car so that if I go to the store, or any place else where there might be a number of adults who would respond to network marketing, I can leave a few tapes or postcards around. My "seeding" was never a mission in itself.

And before you ask, I never got in any trouble for leaving a tape or postcard lying around for someone to discover.

Network Marketing vs. Mail Order

When people are looking at a part–time income business, a lot of them try mail order. Import/export was a big rage for many years, based on the premise that you locate buyers and sellers in foreign countries and act as a middle man, with only a few hours a week invested initially. Mail order has become more popular, and a 1 percent response rate is considered respectable in that business.

When people mention mail order to me, however, even if they have figured out how to do everything over the Internet with their own Website, I point out the percentages. I compare mail order to network marketing. Sure, you can start your own business that way, I say, but the odds are against you. Let's say you're an expert at some hobby or occupation, and you decide to write a book about it, self–publish it in paperback, and do your own marketing. If you sell that book by mail, and you mail out 100 letters and sell three books at $20 each, you've spent all this money on postage and printing and whatever and then you've most likely got a one-time sale to three people, and that's all you've got.

Sure, those people might tell a friend about your book, or order more copies for gifts, but that's nothing. In network marketing if you mail 100 letters and you get three signups, if each one of those three bring you in a few more people, and each one of those bring you a few more people, your one sale in network marketing could be worth an unlimited amount of money.

Let's suppose that in the case of my #1 distributor, rather than selling a network marketing opportunity, I left a tape around promoting a book I'd written. She picked up the tape and listens to it and decides to buy the book, and she sends me $20.

So I've got her $20, and she gets my book.

Instead of that one piece of paper picturing Andrew Jackson, I've made thousands of dollars from my #1 distributor and she has recruited thousands and thousands of people into her downline, all from one plain audio tape left quietly on a chair.

That's the difference in network marketing and mail order or any other part-time business. One response can be worth an unlimited amount of money. Other things are a one-time shot, usually.

More Information Rather Than Less

People like to repeat the phrase "Less is more" and be unobtrusive and polite. That sentiment contributes to my "quiet guy" system. Unfortunately, I'm not the only person who has ever thought of mailing out postcards to mailing lists. There are hundreds of network marketing companies and thousands of individual distributors out there, all mailing out their card stock.

The only effective way to burst through this barrier is to offer more information, and it must come in the form of more details about the company and *proof* that it is actually paying out respectable money to average distributors. That's another reason why my booklet "Secrets of Network Marketing Revealed" worked so well. It had lots of information, and provided a clean statement of the basic principles of the company.

I take every opportunity to drive home why Changes International was the highest–paying, most realistic, easily attainable network marketing opportunity ever. Why not, if it's true? On one flier, I listed the main points so that anyone with a grammar school education could get the picture:

- Beginners and pros are making money fast.
- Experts in the field are saying "WOW!"
- Highest income per person in MLM!
- Deluxe distributor training packs!
- Company does mailing for you for FREE!
- Experienced management.
- Fax on Demand 24 hours a day.
- Checks by FAX or phone accepted. VISA & MasterCard too!
- Low monthly requirement with a two–month grace period.
- Totally unique marketing plan. You've never seen anything like it.
- FASTER PROFIT THAN ANY MLM, PERIOD.
- Ads created by MLM professionals given to you for FREE.

◆ 20-year MLM veterans are saying "This is what I've been waiting for all my life. This answers ALL PREVIOUS MLM PROBLEMS. THIS IS SIMPLY AMAZING!

Do I have to tell you that flier convinced more than a few people to call?

Where To Find Names

As soon as I began having success with Changes International, people called me several times a day to ask how I was able to recruit so many people into the company. Finally, I got smart and made up a two-page flier that explained my methods. One of the first things I emphasized was that you should mail out a booklet instead a postcard whenever possible, despite the extra cost. There's a lot of competition in postcards, I told people, but not nearly as much in mailed booklets.

There are three places I found worthwhile names of prospects. I've already mentioned it, but I want to repeat it again so you don't waste your time with purchased mailing lists, most of which are useless.

1. Most of the material I send out goes to "bounce backs." These are people who sent me network marketing-oriented mail. I don't want onlookers who have little experience in network marketing and do not have a clue as to what to do even if I can get them into a program. I won't turn them away, but if I have to spend money to find people, I want to locate the best people possible. I want *experienced* network marketers, even if they are working another program when I find them, or even if they have failed at several programs like I had prior to Changes. At least they will know the lingo of network marketing, and I won't have to spend half an hour explaining what a downline is and how it works.

2. The next best person to mail to is anyone who advertises in network marketing or mail order publications. Although I vastly prefer network marketing over mail order for reasons previously stated, people who are in the mail order business are actively trying to recruit people via mailings, and thus they fit into my program nicely. Like folks who advertise in network marketing publications, they are risk takers who are willing to spend money to make money, and not lookie–loos trying to gather fuel for a fireplace. One new distributor of mine, who was operating on a very limited budget, went through a network marketing publication and sent out some material on Changes International to the addresses given in a few ads and landed a heavy hitter as a result, one of those Type A born salespersons who helped boom my distributor's business. I cannot guarantee you will land a heavy hitter this way, but you will get a higher caliber of distributors.

3. The third way I get distributors is by... drum roll, please... advertising. I send all my first and second level distributors a list of network marketing publications. In the information they receive, I suggest that they contact each of these publications and get a free sample copy with advertising rates.

Beating the Competition

I'm often asked "What if several of us mail to the same people in network marketing publications?"

My reply? "Great!" I assure them that the vast majority of sales are not closed on the first, second or even third presentation. The majority are closed on something like the sixth or seventh. Remember, the first time I responded to the Changes International ad that said "Now you can earn real MLM money..." it was not the first time I had seen it. A portion of people may respond to the very first mailing they receive, but many will not act until they've received several mailings. If they see something enough times, they start saying to themselves "Something must be going on here if all these people are getting in on this." Personally, when I mail to someone I don't care if they have received something from another Changes distributor or not. I know that the percentages are with me. Sometimes I get a response from my first mailing, so maybe someone else has laid the ground work for me.

In the advertising business, they call this method "making impressions." Each time someone sees a billboard, hears a radio commercial, or sees an ad on TV, it makes an impression. When enough impressions have been made ("enough" varies by individual), they act, if they have any interest at all in the subject. That's why I don't simply mail to people who send me offers just once. I plan on remailing to them five or six times. If they respond before my last mailing, lucky for me.

After I began using audio tapes, the efficacy of making impressions was magnified. Distributors told me that when they followed up paper mailings with an audio tape, they got an immediate reaction and signup. I cannot guarantee this will happen every time, but if you do have a hot prospect or an experienced network marketer on the other line, sending them a tape could mean the difference between landing an effective distributor or not.

Network Marketing Publications & Lead Sources

Network marketing companies come and go, but network marketing publications seem to stay in business longer. The two main magazines that I used to build my business were *Cutting Edge* and *Money and Profits*. *Cutting Edge* was one of the first commercial magazine that geared itself toward network marketing, that made itself a combination of articles and advertising. *Money and Profits* followed, and some others sprang up recently, like *Network Opportunities*. *Money Makers Monthly* has been around a long time and it has a good reputation of giving the most official news on network marketing in general. Whatever magazines you advertise in, just remember that no matter what you say in an ad, if the overall magazine does not present it in a professional way, it won't do you much good.

One of the main problems when you are advertising for network marketing as opposed to regular business opportunities is that most opportunity seekers want to buy something that is going to get them rich (like a postcard system). Companies that offer this type of business are looking for a one–time sale or maybe a follow-up sale, so I mostly stay away from non–network marketing magazines with regard to advertising.

In network marketing, you don't want to merely sell something; **you want to find workers.** You want individuals who are willing to risk their time and money to better their life. They are a different group of people than those who buy into "get rich" schemes. I never have and never will advertise in home–based business or small business publications. You can go to any newsstand and find a half-dozen of these publications. I leave them alone, because ads in those magazines will not bring you network marketing workers, only "get rich quick" people who would often do just as well playing the lottery.

Upline magazine has a good reputation. It covers the type of sales training that people do—how to approach your friends, how to approach your relatives, how to do meetings, etc.

I mainly recommend *Cutting Edge, Money and Profits*, but also *Network Opportunities*. When someone gets into my downline, I usually recommended that they get *Cutting Edge* and *Money and Profits* to get familiar with the business, and I suggest they consider placing ads there first.

I keep a sheet handy of network marketing publications for any of my distributors who want it, with address and phone numbers, but since these publications can go in and out of business only slightly less regularly than new "get rich quick" schemes, I won't bother listing them here.

Future Developments

In the beginning, I think my first few levels of distributors relied primarily on my recommendations and advice for their promotional business activities. In the winter of 1995 through spring of 1996, I was selling around ten copies of my three-step system per day. These days, there are people who get into Changes International who know nothing about my system, who get in for the age–old reason—someone talks them into it. I don't even know if a majority of them even realize the importance of the Changes pay plan. They just get in because somebody said that this was the latest thing.

The truth is, the value of any system only lasts for so long, and after a while it starts to wane because it is no longer innovative. My system does not work nearly as well as it did in the first year, because when something has been around a while, people get used to it, take it for granted, and even copy your methods. That certainly happened with the Changes International pay plan. Additionally, one person who will go unnamed here copied my mail order system. He wrote a booklet, he made that booklet available to his downline, and he provided coop mailing of the booklet.

One big problem. The pay plan of the company he works with stunk, forcing him to fall back on old methods of really working people hard to get them to go to meetings, and drilling them mercilessly to get them to stay in.

No matter what I tell you, or anyone else tells you, no matter how tried and true any method is, it may lose effectiveness as it becomes widely known. The basic principles of human behavior may not change much, but people are not stupid. They like to see and try something new. If it happens to make a great deal of sense and offer a level of fairness that never existed before, as did the Changes International pay plan when it was first developed, it is nevertheless inevitable that you will develop your own unique way of implementing any 100 percent turnkey system. Since I don't know you or what you're really all about, I can only outline my own personal evolution, and relate how I refined my own system to make it as absolutely 100 percent workable as possible for anyone in my downline. By showing you how I developed my system, maybe I'll give you some ideas of other methods you can use to become a highly successful network marketer in your own special way.

6

HOW MY SYSTEM EVOLVED

When someone gets into network marketing, the way to success is not to approach it with the idea "What can I do to get rich?" Instead, you should continually ask yourself "What can I do to help my downline?" When I wrote the booklet "Secrets of Network Marketing Plans Revealed," I didn't decide one day, "I need to write a booklet so I can get rich." I realized I needed to create something that my downline could use that would explain how other companies presented their network marketing plans in ways that deceived people. If I could put the numbers and facts and percentages on paper in a simple, easily understood way, that sales tool would lead people into signing up with Changes.

And that's what I did. The idea was not to sit down and think what I could do to become rich, but what I could do to help my downline, in a way that would enable them to help others understand.

Motivational speaker Zig Ziglar, a regular speaker at network marketing conventions, said: "You can get everything in life you want if you will just help enough other people get what they want."

Boy, is that ever true. I didn't give anyone false hopes; I stressed that the check amounts I received were not an inducement or a guarantee of what an average distributor would earn. Nevertheless, it made sense to anyone who had been involved with any previous network marketing company that usually only 10 percent or so of the people at the top make money, and then only $5 or $10 a distributor. I laid out the facts of how I had done with Changes: my first check was $678 with 22 distributors; my second was $1,300 with 43 distributors; my third was $2,710.86 with 80 distributors. That was just over $30 per distributor, and then they saw that my fourth check was for $5,5010.50, my sixth check for $10,625.29, and my tenth check was $21,059.00. All of this with only a $100 per month purchase necessary on my part. The figures were indisputable, and in the beginning I was always willing to send someone a photocopy of one of my checks to prove it.

On the opposite side of my "Proof" sheet I listed Income Testimonials of real people, with their full names, location and phone numbers (I had their permission, naturally). Remember what I mentioned earlier about the use of testimonials? I had all sorts of people involved in my Changes International downline.

The Changes International Compensation Plan

At this point, it might be wise to explain the pay plan that revolutionized network marketing, the one so many critics said could not work. Its greatest power was its simplicity. To this day, new Changes distributors are given one sheet in the marketing materials they initially receive which explain the entire system. Here it is.

Every new distributor's first question is how much can they expect to earn? It depends on the people they recruit, naturally, but let's say a new person develops a total growthline of twelve individuals:

(a) four personally sponsored on their first level; and

(b) two each recruited by their first–level distributors (making 8 distributors on their second–level).

All of these distributors, to stay active in the program, are purchasing $112 worth of product ($100 Business Volume, or BV) each month, which qualifies them to receive their commission. To qualify for commission, everyone—including the initial distributor, must purchase six bottles of product each month. If the distributor or their family members are not personally using the products, by selling just four bottles each month they cover their monthly purchase obligation. (These examples are based on executive status and not guarantees of income; they simply represent potential earnings.)

Changes pays 15 percent on the distributor's first–level business volume and 45 percent on the second. Here's how the commission is calculated:

4 first–level distributors x $15 commission (15% of their business volume) = $60 (first–level commission)

8 second–level distributors x $45 commission each (45% of their $100 business volume) = $360 (second–level commission).

Under this scenario, the distributor's total commission for the month would be $420, also qualifying them for an Leadership Bonus (formerly called the "Infinity Bonus").

Now, let say they personally sponsor 12 executives, who each sponsored eight? 12 first–level x $15 commission = $180. 96 second–level distributors x $45 = $4,320. The distributor would be earning $4,500 for the month—and their Leadership Bonus would bump it up even more.

With the Third Level to Leadership Bonus, early efforts are well rewarded, which is music to the ears of anyone afraid that people in their downline may kick back and relax after recruiting a few first-level distributors.

The Third Level to Leadership Bonus is an incentive for people to continually, personally recruit more people who will sell products, and thus qualify high producers for incrementally larger commission checks.

The bonus is calculated according to rank:

1–Star Executive:	Reached by personally sponsoring 3 people who each purchase/sell $100BV of products every month.
2–Star Executive:	6 people.
3–Star Executive:	9 people.
4–Star Executive:	12 personally sponsored people.

Third Level to Leadership bonuses vary by Star Executive ranking and how many Star Executives are below the distributor in question. This bonus is shared with the Star Executives below. If a 4-Star Executive qualifies to receive a 15 percent bonus and has a 2-Star Executive below him, he receives 15 percent on the sales of everyone above that 2-Star Executive and 8 percent on the sales below that Executive. As you can see, there are many possible Leadership Bonus scenarios, but the main point is that those who produce, and get others to produce, are well rewarded.

Many distributors (such as myself) soon found that the Leadership Bonus began accounting for two-thirds of their total commission.

So that's a simple description of the Changes pay plan. For me, it isn't hard to understand even without a chart. If you've ever tried to make sense of some of those terribly confusing charts of other network marketing companies, I'm sure you understand exactly what I mean.

My Booming Business Problem

Almost without exception, most distributors were able to understand the Changes pay plan and implement the marketing system I developed with little problem. My main dilemma, as my business took off, was answering the same questions over and over when people in my downline called. I began getting too few hours of sleep, which started to infringe upon my health.

I wasn't sure what to do about the situation until I reread one of the fliers I created for my people listing things network marketers don't know:

1. POTENTIAL PAYOUT MEANS NOTHING! (Except for heavy hitters.)

2. Unless you are an experienced, professional network marketer you will never come close to the "potential" payout.

3. The only thing that counts for you is what the company pays out to its distributors "ON AVERAGE."

4. Any mathematician or Las Vegas gambler will tell you you are ALWAYS BETTER TO GO WHERE THE **ODDS ARE IN YOUR FAVOR**. TO BE A SUCCESSFUL NETWORK MARKETER, BE A WISE & INFORMED NETWORK MARKETER

One morning as I was trying to shake the sleep out of my eyes, while drinking a cup of coffee and listening to the answering machine pick up yet another call, I looked at item (4) above and wondered how I could improve the odds that yet another distributor would not call me with a question I had answered only minutes before.

That's when it hit me. I had no trouble explaining things so my downline could understand, if my booklet was any indication. Wasn't I telling folks to be a wise and informed network marketer? Maybe I just wasn't informing them often enough?

That was it. I kept myself informed about network marketing by constantly reading and studying new ideas, which I then passed on to my distributors, in phone call after phone call. Sure, they could inform the people in their downline what I'd said, but things changed day to day, week to week, month to month. My booklet and the tapes certainly didn't cover everything, and I couldn't stay on top of every distributor's life to make sure they were reading magazines I suggested and following steps I recommended.

I suspected I was getting so many phone calls because lots of distributors thought I had some magic secret that they could only get by speaking to me personally. And why not? I'd had a similar opinion when involved in other network marketing companies, that there was some secret I just hadn't found yet. When getting involved in Changes, I'd called Scott Paulsen and talked to him a long time. Maybe my people were calling so much because they were afraid of being left out of the loop?

I realized then I needed something else, a regular way of keeping my people informed and taking care of their needs. I needed to send out regular newsletters.

My Downline Letters

Starting in 1995, I began sending out letters to all my distributors on a monthly basis, to keep them informed of: (a) changes in the company; (b) my feelings about new products and ideas, and (c) successes of other people in my downline. The letters turned out to be so popular that after awhile, at the insistence of distributors, I began to offer a bound sheaf of them entitled "The Best of Joe Brown's Downline Letters." I include those letters here, with some cosmetic changes and notes so that readers unfamiliar to network marketing terms will not be confused. I hope they help paint a detailed picture of some of the struggles and triumphs we had in building our success. These letters were another vital part of how I created my own workable system, and may give you some ideas of how to structure and implement your own methods of building a business. Note: I do not include here attachments that went with these letters.

Also, these letters show that even with success, you will have problems, and you must learn how to deal with them.

If you're relatively new to network marketing, by studying the concerns addressed in these letters, you might gain some insight into the type of problems that I've seen pop up in many network marketing companies. And who knows? By reading about some of the problems we faced, such as a negative review in a magazine and how we dealt with it, you might even get some laughs.

❖   ❖   ❖   ❖   ❖

August 23rd, 1995
There seem to be people out there who have paranoia about being "blocked out," or prevented from contin-

uing to expand their income as more people come into their downline. This is true in theory, but at this time only 5 percent of all distributors are achieving the four-star status, so we will be paid on the vast majority of our downline. I am getting paid from 15 levels deep with a 67 percent activity rate. These numbers are astronomical in this business. This activity rate is actually higher because of the people who come in at the end of the month and do not order products (they usually wait for the first of the month to actually begin) and the computer lists them as inactive. So, if new or potential distributors are concerned about being "blocked-out," it's because they can't see the GIANT FOREST for a tiny twig of a tree!

Please pass this important information on to your downline!

Also, I have many distributors calling and asking me about tapes, artwork and various questions they should have received from their sponsors.

I would also like to share some information regarding the psychology of the business, or belief, or whatever you wish to call it. In January 1995, when I signed up with Changes, I did not know that it would really take off like this. But I did expect to sign up distributors quite easily. I believed I could get 12 front line distributors, not because of my ability to recruit, but because I really believed in this compensation plan.

I knew that anyone who had experienced the frustration of trying to build a profitable organization with plans that paid 5 percent to 10 percent per level would immediately realize the tremendous potential of this company which pays 45 percent on the second level. So I was not surprised when people began to sign up rapidly. This may sound like motivation "hype" but if you want to sign up lots of distributors, you have to expect that you will. In every book I have ever read on success, the authors will tell you that the main ingredient to success is expecting, not hoping or wishing but EXPECTING your dream will come true.

❖   ❖   ❖

September 20, 1995
I get calls almost every day from distributors asking me questions that have already been answered in these letters. It is not that what I have to say this time is any more urgent than previous letters, but you may be losing out on business when your downline lacks information. So PLEASE pass this and all letters on down. I CANNOT mail to 2,600 people.

Although I am not sending out copies of my checks any more, I am enclosing a copy of my downline report. The chief reason for this is that many experienced network marketers do not believe this marketing plan pays DEEP. They are paranoid about being "blocked out" after they have 12 distributors somewhere and think they won't get paid deep.

As you can see, not only am I getting paid 15 levels deep [downline report omitted], but the Leadership Bonus is a WHOPPING 62 percent of my check. When I first got in, I did not know how this Leadership Bonus would pay. I looked on it as possible icing on the cake. Was I surprised! My Leadership Bonus keeps growing each time and yours will too. So, if you come across some "hitter" who thinks he or she will not make the money deep, then show them this. Another point to remember is that you have to have 12 PERSONALLY SPONSORED people before you get blocked out. The company statistics are that only 5 percent of all distributors are earning the four-star position.

THIS PAY PLAN DOES PAY DEEP AND IT IS VERY FINANCIALLY LUCRATIVE—DON'T LET ANYONE TELL YOU OTHERWISE!

I get reports every week from people in my downline who have "bounced back" on an offer sent to them and get a higher caliber distributor. Some of these people have nice downlines in other companies. Your check will grow much faster if you can land "experienced" people than by going after new and inexperienced people from mailing lists.

One more thing to remind you. This marketing plan is working the way plans are supposed to work. In the month of August I personally sponsored only 12 people, but my downline grew from 1,350 to almost 2,600. You will not find any other marketing plan on earth that can remotely come close to this. Once you get a little group working under you, your checks will also begin to TAKE OFF!

Do our products work? When the testimonial tapes come out in October, you will hear about one person, who lost an astronomical 88 pounds in 20 weeks simply by taking the Thermo–Lift. Plus, you'll hear many other powerful testimonials on our other products.

I appreciate everyone's diligent work that is helping me make more money in one month than I made in a YEAR for most of my life.

❖ ❖ ❖

November 23, 1995
I am writing this letter on Thanksgiving because that is the only time I have when the phone is not ringing constantly. So on to the business at hand.

The computer is not breaking the report down between the 1st and 2nd levels and the Leadership Bonus. But the Leadership Bonus is continually becoming a larger part of the check. Many distributors are losing out on commissions because while their downline is growing, they do not have enough 1st level people to reap the rewards of this amazing marketing plan.

The situation I would like to address this month is drop outs. We all have them. What can we do?

I have found that the main reason people drop out is because they are still mailing postcards and are getting little results. I have said all along that although I did have some success in mailing postcards in the beginning, I soon realized that you need more information to convince people to take a look at Changes. You must explain to them the "hows" and "whys" of the marketing plan and the reasons it is so much more lucrative than anything out there. This is why I created all of the support material. It is amazing to me that I have several calls every day from new distributors who have not heard one single thing about the booklet, the voice mail, or anything else in the artwork package that is working so well. If you are not spreading this information to your downline, you cannot expect results. Postcards by themselves WILL NOT WORK. You must have support materials.

The people in my downline that are having real success are mailing out the booklet, *Secrets of Network Marketing Plans Revealed*. It also amazes me that even those who have not heard about this have no idea how to get it, what it costs or anything. It seems like 99 percent of all new distributors or prospects are simply told to call me for all the information. This is not network marketing. You are supposed to pass the information down. When new distributors continue to mail out only postcards and cannot get through to me on the phone to ask the same questions that are already available in print or on the audio tape, it is no wonder that they drop out. I think a lot of new distributors are told just to get in and everything else works like magic.

This is important. My phone rings all day with new distributors asking the same questions over and over again. Then each night I have about 10 to 20 calls from people with the same questions. I don't have time to call all of these people back. So either they don't get it or they don't know what to do. It is no wonder that we have dropouts. Our drop out rate is still much much less than any other network marketing company I have heard of, but think how much larger your check would be if more people stayed in because they had the correct information and *they* recruited more people because *they* had the correct information.

Probably the number one question I get asked over and over again is who to mail to and where to get leads. So at the constant urging of many in my downline, I have decided to get into a lead–generating program. [THAT LEAD COMPANY IS NOW CLOSED.] We all need leads and many do not get enough mail to do the bounce backs effectively.

❖   ❖   ❖

January 9, 1996
I have an idea I would like to share that should enable us to tap a more qualified group of distributors. We have all experienced recruiting new distributors who are full of excitement, only to find out that they gave up after a few short months. So let's go after those who are more long–term, goal–oriented and do not give up so easily.

Pick up the latest copy of *Success* magazine (December 1995). The lead article is about network marketing and is very positive. It shows that network marketing is becoming more respectable and many high caliber and professional individuals are getting involved. Many are leaving the corporate world and are earning good money in network marketing.

I plan to set up a voice mail box with a little pitch about the benefits and the income possibilities of network marketing. Here is what I suggest: have them leave their name and address on a voice mail box and then send them a photocopy of the article from *Success* magazine and some very professional-looking information on Changes.

The article from *Success* will give credibility to network marketing and Changes will give them the tool. If you read this article in *Success*, it states that those who have been really successful in this business go after professionals—not the average, every day network marketer who chases every whim of an opportunity and gives up so easily. If we can get some of these higher-caliber people in our downline, I am sure our checks will increase dramatically.

I am sharing this idea with you before I have tested it myself. I will let you know next month what happened and I would appreciate hearing from anyone about their success. This letter is going out to every Changes distributor I have an address for, but this will be the last letter anyone gets from me unless it is specifically requested.

I have given up on trying to get my first level to pass information down. One of the key rules in successful management is sharing as much information with those who work with you—not hoarding it because of some type of power trip.

I am tired of having people angry at me because they do not have information that should have come from their upline. Several times, this has made me look like an upline who just does not care or who is sharing information with certain "favorite" people.

I am looking forward to a very positive and profitable year with Changes. The company is still very young. Many professional network marketers will not even look at a company until it is three to five years old. Just think where we will all be on the income picture if we hang in there until the really big growth starts to happen. Changes has caused quite a ruckus in the industry and we are getting loads of distributors from several other big name network marketing companies. The company is a growing force to be reckoned with.

I hope you make more money this year than you ever thought realistically possible.

❖ ❖ ❖

February 25, 1996
Several times each week I talk to distributors who have two different types of experiences. Some are very excited about the results they are having and some are frustrated.

I am continuously asked exactly what I am doing. So I will go over that and you can compare with your marketing efforts. Probably the most common question I get is "how many" I am mailing each week or month and exactly what it is that I am mailing.

The answer to that is basically, I do not do very much straight out mailing to lists and names. The majority of my marketing efforts come from filling individual requests for information packs that are the results of my advertising.

The publications that I use most are *Cutting Edge* and *Money & Profits*. But there are many others and I try these from time to time. I DO NOT KEEP TRACK OF RESULTS! So please don't ask. I just try to get a feel of how the ad is doing. I have stayed out of *Cutting Edge* and *Money & Profits* to allow other distributors to use these, but I get results when there are other Changes ads, too. And I get results from other publications also.

I spend my money advertising, rather than using lists, because it is more time-effective and I am mailing to only those who have expressed interest in my ad. I probably send out six or so packages each day. If they send me money or stamps I send them the *Secrets* booklet, the original sponsoring tape, the company brochure & application (copied) and about two or three pages of testimonials. (These are a combination of product and income.) I think I usually sign up about four to six distributors a month, but this is only a guess and it may vary. If they do not send me money or stamps I simply send them the booklet. If they cannot send me $3 or ten stamps, I am not going to waste money on them. If they write me a note and seem interested, I will enclose more information.

The other main source of my marketing efforts comes from "bounce backs." I have continually stressed this and it is still working. These people who mail you stuff have identified themselves as workers. They are willing to spend their money in recruiting efforts. So if you can turn these people around, they will work for you. Still, I only get a very small percentage, but once you have one, you usually have an experienced and knowledgeable downline member and you don't have to spend a lot of time training them.

I usually mail these people a *Secrets* booklet, but if they have sent me a nice package, and especially if they have sent me a tape, I will send them a larger package back. The more they spend trying to get you means the more they will spend working for you, if you can turn them around.

A few weeks ago, I signed up a distributor from another company who had a pretty good downline. All I did was "bounce back" with the booklet and he was really impressed with what it revealed to him. So there are hard-working distributors out there who have good downlines but still don't understand the significance of marketing plans.

On that subject, in a discussion with Scott [Paulsen] the other day, he mentioned that Changes is having a large influx of "former" distributors who are coming back in. Again, this gets back to the "theory" of network marketing versus the "reality" of network marketing. People get called and some fast- talking distributor from some other company bends their ear about some hot new product or some new company pay plan which is supposedly "much better" than Changes. After a few months the reality factor steps in and the distributor realizes he has been taken by the hype and decides to get back into Changes.

This influx of former distributors is such a great selling point when someone is trying to recruit you into their "hot" program. Simply tell them we have had distributors try other programs and now they are coming back in. This says something very powerful about our marketing plan.

Scott mentioned this in the latest newsletter, but I am going to repeat it because it is so important. We are growing fast and a large percentage of orders come in the last few days of the month and first few of the next month. So please try and place your product order at other times during the month to avoid a delay, or simply sign up for the automatic order.

Also, Scott and I are having to deal with a similar problem. I mentioned this in my last newsletter, but I will mention it again. You CANNOT get a new distributor in and tell them "I don't know much, but just call Joe or Scott and they will answer all of your questions." You must learn all about Changes from your sponsor so you can help your new people. This is what network marketing is all about.

Sure, we are here to answer difficult questions, or maybe talk to a potential heavy-hitter, but most of the questions you should be able to handle yourself or with your sponsor. THIS IS IMPORTANT. Please don't tell new people to call me or the company unless you have gone to your sponsor and several levels up in your upline to get an answer.

Back to marketing.

Testimonials, testimonials. Nothing sells like testimonials. Every company has a few big distributors who are making good money. But most new people want to know what the average person is doing. I am willing to share with everyone what I am making because it shows the potential of this pay plan. But what everyone needs is as many testimonials from other distributors as you can possibly get your hands or ears on. That is why I mentioned before that in my pack I have (I just counted them) 10 pages—that's 5 pages, back to back, of product and income testimonials. This just dawned on me as I write—maybe that is why I get better results from my recruiting efforts than many others. Sure, I tell them what I have done, but I also want any new prospect to know that we have many others doing well also.

Years ago (for a very short time) I was a salesman for Combined Insurance Company. This company was started by W. Clement Stone. He made millions during the Depression selling insurance. How was he able to do this? I will tell you because I was trained in their system. We salesmen would walk down the street, going into one retail establishment after another. We would walk in and speak to the manager or owner. When we had their attention, we brought out this huge three-ring binder and started showing them something. Did we start talking insurance? No. We showed them name after name after name of other retailers in the area who had purchased insurance from us. Here is where the magic, mystical esoteric event takes place.

These retailers saw all these names of people and establishments who had decided to go with us. This made them realize: "All these successful people can't be wrong. They must be doing something right. I want to be like them, so I want to get in on this." In human psychology, there is a feeling of safety when you are part of a group. That is why so many infomercials are filled with testimonials and famous people if they can get them. Madison Avenue marketing experts fully understand the **awesome power of testimonials!**

So, my suggestion is to get with your upline or downline and collect as many income and product testimonials as you can and get them down on paper so that you can mail these out or read them over the phone when you are talking with people. If you do this, I am absolutely sure it will make a big difference in your recruiting efforts.

My check for January was $29,000. $5,000 from the first three levels and $24,000 from the Leadership Bonus. So don't let anyone tell you that their marketing plan is better or that you are going to "lose out" on the Leadership Bonus. This brings to mind what one supposed "expert" in network marketing plans said in his review of Changes a few months ago. This is not an exact quote, but it went something like: "The Changes pay plan can earn you some money quicker than most pay plans on the first two levels, but you will never make any significant money on the Leadership Bonus." Eat your heart out, expert. I challenge anyone in all of network marketing to make this kind of money, all by mail, without meetings or spending nights or weekends on the phone.

I appreciate all of your efforts. The ideas and courage of Scott and Terry Paulsen who had the wisdom, insight and (most of all) courage to go against the pack and create this company when everyone said it would not work... and all of you distributors who are working hard in your spare time have changed my life in a way that I thought was only possible in my wildest dreams.

❖   ❖   ❖

March 28, 1996
I am running a 40-word [a small ad] in a very specialized card deck that goes only to individuals who run small business or who have shown an interest in starting one from home. These have been qualified several different ways to eliminate "lookie-loos," the vast majority of people whose part-time hobby is getting junk mail. These new individuals should be the type of people we want. I will need your feedback on how good these leads are.

The long term view of Changes. Changes has grown so fast recently there have been product delay problems and mix-ups. No one denies this has happened, but I urge everyone to keep a long-term view in mind. I wish everyone had the opportunity to talk with Scott and Terry as much as I do. Then you would know, as I know, that they are definitely in this for the long term. Scott is a very capable business person. He has planned for growth but Changes has simply taken off a little faster than projected. Just remember, they have never been late with the checks and they have plans for additional products.

We are still very small by network marketing standards. I sincerely believe we will be a major network marketing company in a few years and those of us who are in now will benefit tremendously from this. We are now entering the momentum stage and heavy hitters who have been sitting on the sidelines watching are beginning to come in and bring in hundreds, if not thousands, of distributors with them.

Some people have wondered if it is too late to make good money with Changes. Here are two different examples. I spoke to one super heavy-hitter a few months ago who makes $60,000 per month and he told me he never gets into a company unless it is at least five years old!! I spoke to a new Changes distributor who just got in who was not a hitter and he got a $600+ check his first month. I put an ad in my local paper the first of January for someone to help me with the phones, etc. In the ad I said "some knowledge of Network Marketing a plus." Out of over 30 phone calls I received, only ONE PERSON, that's one person out of 30, even knew what network marketing is! There are millions and jillions of people out there who HAVE NEVER HEARD OF NETWORK MARKETING. So don't let ANYONE tell you it's too late to get into Changes.

Then there is another distributor who lives in Mesa, Arizona. He got into Changes on December 17th, 1995 and signed up twelve people before the end of the year. Right in the midst of Christmas season, when you are not supposed to be able to do this. By the way, He is 80 YEARS OLD!!!

When new potential distributors call me about Changes, I do not get into discussions about products, milligrams, ingredients, I just simply say OVER AND OVER AGAIN "We have the absolute best marketing plan in the business." I just push the marketing plan. Distributors call and ask about ingredients, comparisons, approvals, what some company is doing, and on and on. I don't get involved in any of this stuff.

People ask me what I am doing to be successful. I just talk about the marketing plan. That is what sets us apart from every

other company out there and that's what really counts.

I know many of you are detail and perfection buffs. And that is good if that is your personality. But that's not me. I am a very unorganized person who misses some of the details. I just push the marketing plan.

I never imagined that developing a system that would work by mail would involve making my phone ring all day long without stopping. I love this company and I love the money, but the phone sometimes drives me crazy. Yes, I have tried hiring other people to do some of my personal work, but it does not get done right. And so many people who call insist on talking to me.

❖   ❖   ❖

May 24, 1996
Changes is still growing at 35 percent per month! Call any professional business organization and ask them how difficult it would be to maintain a business growth of 35 percent per month. They will tell you that it is phenomenal, and that any owner or manager that could keep a business up and running at that pace must be close to a business genius. Please keep this in mind if you do experience mixups or delays.

Herbalife went through a time like this and those who stuck it out are millionaires. So let's all keep the long term picture in mind. There is simply no opportunity on the face of the Earth where an average individual can make the kind of money we can make without years of experience and training.

Yes, I know it gets frustrating when you don't get product or there is a mix-up in your order, but remember, this is a short-term situation, and even if it does not get resolved immediately, those checks just keep coming getting larger and don't forget this—THE CHECKS HAVE ALWAYS COME ON TIME!

We have a money–making machine here. We have... 1.) The most lucrative and fastest pay plan ever, 2.) Great products with never–ending testimonials, 3.) Powerful marketing and recruiting tapes, and 4.) A proven and easily duplicatable 3-step mail order system.

Since I have continually gotten my best results from bounce backs and my own ads, I am changing my focus. It is my belief that we are much better off when people respond to ads specifically for Changes. Although I never mention the company name, I always use descriptions that set us apart from other network marketing companies. I believe that people who answer simple generic ads like... "Make a fortune working from your home," are more the "lookie–loo, tire kicker" types than real network marketing workers.

❖ ❖ ❖

June 15, 1996
This time I want to talk a little about focus. I know this may sound like a rerun of something you have heard or read many times. I have read this many times myself and put it in the category in my mind called "general and vague principles."

It was only when I began to look closely over my recent downline report did I realize how significant focus is. As I looked over the names and the number of distributors they had, it almost jumped out that those individuals who have continually and steadily worked Changes had much larger downlines, and thus larger checks, than those who did not.

How do I know the ones who did not? Because I have received mailings and phone calls from these people giving me the pitch on some other program. Now, I am not so judgmental on this because I have been in the same boat and I was always looking for a "better deal." We are by nature risk takers and are ready to jump at something that looks like fast money.

The difference now is that there simply is not anything better. In my discussions with new and present distributors, I continually bring the conversation back to the marketing plan. There are always going to be new companies and hot products springing up. You can be sure I hear about all of them. But in everything I see there is simply no comparison to our marketing plan.

When you are talking with potential prospects, don't get sidetracked on milligrams, absorption rates, subjective comparisons, or which acre of land some product comes from. If someone wants to get into a big discussion about some of these things, I tell them to go down to their local health food store and see what they can find. But if they are looking for the best business opportunity around, there simply is no comparison.

So let's keep focused on Changes as a company and our marketing plan. The simple truth is that if you spend time on anything else, your check will not go up that fast. I have heard from several distributors over the past few months who have chased something else for a while, only to come back, dragging their tails behind them, realizing that THERE REALLY IS NOTHING BETTER.

Thank you for your continued hard work.

❖   ❖   ❖

July 23, 1996
People continually ask me what the "secret" was to my success in Changes. To repeat the same story: I basically copied the company's original full page ad, MAILED MAILED MAILED and MAILED SOME MORE, while continuing to improve on the 3-step system. While this is all very important, there is something

much more important in the overall scheme of things. Next time I will write about the **belief** that you can succeed, which is the *most important principle of all* regarding your own personal success.

WHAT DOES JOE MAIL?
Unbelievable, yes, but we get this one all the time. We send the booklet to names from lead programs, to bounce-backs (counter–offers) and advertise (almost entirely in network marketing publications) that people can get a free booklet from us or a larger info kit for $3 or 10 stamps (which helps weed out the lookie–loos). Sometimes we send out postcards to test questionable mailing lists, but mainly, it's BOOKLET BOOKLET BOOKLET.

DISTRIBUTOR ERRORS
This comes straight from the top of the company. Approximately 70-80 percent of all occasions when a distributor calls in to Changes thinking the company has made an error, it is the *distributor's mistake.* It is surprising, but true. It would really help the company (which in turn helps all of us) if everyone could completely research their problem before calling the company. (Check your distributor application agreement, call your direct upline etc.) And if it becomes absolutely necessary to contact the company, it's always better to FAX a letter instead of calling.

❖   ❖   ❖

September, 1996
One distributor is having good response from running the following ad in *Penny Saver* and *Thrifty Nickel*, etc. [local free newspapers filled mostly with no–cost classified ads]:

"If you have failed in network marketing before, it is not your fault."

The only people who respond to an ad like this have been in network marketing and know what it is.

Since we cannot use specific income testimonials any more, I am stressing in my letters and phone conversations the fact that our CPA firm told us that over a two-year period, from July 1994 to July 1996, we have recruited 50,000 people and 37,000 are still active. That is a 75 percent two-year activity rate, the norm being 10-15 percent per year. Why are so many people sticking with Changes over any other company? People are staying in BECAUSE WE ARE MAKING MONEY. All the hype about potential payouts and Space Age products don't mean a thing if people are not staying in your downline. Let's use logic to combat all of the erroneous hype. You simply cannot argue with the FACTS. Tell this to all potential distributors.

Now here is where I go out on a limb to express some personal thoughts about things. I am continually asked what I did to get such a great start with CHANGES. Even though I have given the mechanics of what I have done, there is more to it.

Last month I talked about getting into a state of mind where you really believe that it is okay to have lots of money. I believe that there are a lot of us who might say: "Sure, I believe that it is a good thing for me to be wealthy," but that is a conscious statement and there is a subconscious part of our mind that does not think so. I have read this in so many books that I believe that this is true. This is something you will have to sort out for yourself. If you do think this is the case with you, then I suggest you fill your mind with stories of people who have done good with their money and that, over time will have an effect on the subconscious.

Again, the reason I have come to believe this is because I have read it in so many success-oriented books and heard it in so many tapes through the years. I am a slow learner—I guess it took years to sink in and take effect.

I can tell you of another very successful, professional network marketer who has done the same thing. I have known him for years by way of my tape business. He is an avid success and prosperity tape junkie and has listened to almost everyone out there. (You can get a lot of these through the Nightingale/ Conant Corp. of Chicago.) Filling his mind with this material has worked for him. The last time we talked, he was making about $80,000 a month.

All these books and tapes will tell you that it is so important to fill your mind with success and prosperity-oriented thoughts and ideas. You have to do this to break through to the subconscious and program yourself for success and prosperity.

> *Note: The following portion of this letter is very important. I believe it is one of the key elements to my success and could be a key to your success also. This emphasis was not included in my original letter to the people in my downline.*

Now this brings up another point, that may seem a little more far out: the LAW OF ATTRACTION. Simply defined, it means that what you put out is what you get back, or what you spend your time thinking about is what you bring into your life. This is important. If you have bills and you spend your time worrying about those bills, that is what you will attract. More bills! Even if you spend your time thinking about how much you dislike the bills or don't want them, the more you spend thinking. about them, the more you will get.

Again, if you worry about getting into a car accident or worry about your relationship or what "could" go wrong at the job, that is what you will get—so think about positive things, not negative.

If you think that this is a bunch of metaphysical-sounding psychology, I will tell you that all successful people speak about this in one way or another. Personally, it took me years to accept this. In fact, I was the utmost skeptic.

❖ ❖ ❖

October 29, 1996
One question I am frequently asked is "is it too late to get into Changes?"

There are two answers to this question: 1.) Amway and Shaklee have been around for thirty years and they are still recruiting people. So we have barely scratched the surface; 2.) A lot of people in mail order have heard about Changes, so the potential for growth may not be quite as fast, but we now have the stability. When I first got in, very few were willing to take a chance on a new company.

This leads me to a conclusion. Now is the time to go after the more professional crowd. Each year *Success* magazine devotes an entire issue to network marketing. It is getting more positive each year. The main thrust of these articles is that network marketing is rapidly gaining ground as not only an acceptable method to do business, but one of the best opportunities to obtain financial independence. These issues are full of examples of individuals who have left the stress-filled, deadline-dominated life of the executive/professional world and are now happily and prosperously working a network marketing company.

Think about this. These high-powered professional types are happy working some program with the typical, crummy marketing plan and doing very well. What if they heard about Changes and our marketing plan? What if they realized they could be making 3-4 times that?

Another point found in these articles is that the thought of "being their own boss" and "having their own time on working according to their own schedule" is just as important than the money. With this in mind, I want to present some ideas about how to go after these professionals:

Although I have never encouraged putting ads in regular newspapers because you get so many people looking for a job, let's attack it from another angle. Put an ad in the largest city paper in your area, under investment opportunities:

"Professionals or business owners only. Double or triple your income this year. We have many individuals with little or no experience making six figure incomes. Our company has one of the highest percentage of successful individuals of any company in our field. Minimal investment. Call or write..."

When they call, rather than giving them the big pitch right away, you want to use a technique that makes them even more interested. You want to qualify them. So when they ask "What this is about?" you say "I'll explain it in a moment, but first, I would like to ask a few questions. This is not for everyone." (Key phrase, they immediately want to be accepted as one of the chosen few.)

Here are some questions.

> "Are you a professional in some field or do you own your own business?"

(Let them tell you how qualified they are.)

"Can you handle responsibility comfortably?"

"Can you work on your own without supervision?"

"Would you like to have more time and work on your own schedule?"

"If you are accepted can you commit at least three months to see if this will work for you?"

Once they have answered yes to these questions, you want to start on something like this: "I represent a 2-1/2 year old company that is setting our industry on fire. We have people who do not have the skills or training you obviously have, who are making six figure incomes working part time. And some of our more successful people will make close to half a million dollars this year."

Remember, nothing sells like testimonials. Now, I know that we can't make specific claims in print, but we can tell people what the potential is when talking to them.

Then I would mention *Success* magazine and the articles they have each year on "our type" of business and how so many executive types are leaving their high pressure world to do this type of business. Then say: "But there is one big difference. Our company pays two to four times as much as the companies they are working with and they are happy. Think how much better off we are."

All this time, you want to avoid like the plague the words "network marketing" or "health products." If they hear these words before you give them the testimonials and credibility info, they will quickly jump to a preconceived conclusion.

But after you have gone through the preceding guidelines, then you can tell them about the company and what we do. If they say "I'm not into health products" you can come back with two things: "The health products are only a vehicle that works well with this type of business. For example, you must have a monthly reorder type of product. And, the health and weight loss business is one of the fastest-growing industries today. It grows substantially each year."

The rest is up to you. I have presented this as if you had these prospects calling you. But if you feel uncomfortable about this, I have come up with a letter that follows those exact guidelines, and can be mailed to those who answer your ad. If you do it this way, do not, I repeat, DO NOT send anything else to them other than the letter. No booklets, product info or anything. They must read the letter from start to finish in the order I have given and then at the bottom, you can say something like: "If you are really serious about checking into this and can commit to at least three months, then call or write..."

Let's back up. Since you have to put this ad under "Business Investments" they are going to ask: "What is the investment?" You say, the major investment is your own time, but there is a minimal purchase of $100 your first month. After that you should be well ahead of the game. If you're not, then this business is not for you."

So where else can we place ads like this? I have seen them in the *Wall Street Journal*, *Investors Business Daily*, *Business Week*. Look for card decks that go out to professionals or executives only. Don't make the false conclusion that all these big guns are making so much money they would turn their nose up at a $100,000+ additional yearly income.

Here is another idea for an ad heading.

"Downsized out of a job?"

"Making good money but hate the rat race?"

"Middle management laid off?"

"Love the money but hate your boss?"

"Lady professionals, had it to the fill with your male chauvinist inferior who has the title of 'superior'?"

After each of these you want to go back to the original starting with "professionals or business owners only..."

There is a world of high-caliber people out there who would give anything for the opportunity we have. All we have to do is make them aware of it and then back it up with the facts of the growing credibility of network marketing and testimonials of those who are succeeding.

I hope this letter has helped. I would appreciate any feedback from those of you who try the professional approach.

❖   ❖   ❖

November, 1996

You can always learn a lot from the experiences of successful people. I was listening to some tapes by Tony Robbins and he said he was asked why he thought he was so much more successful than the average person. He replied, "I worked a lot harder and I expected to succeed." He talked about when he was 17 years old and he got a job selling motivational tapes. The person he worked for required that each employee had to purchase his $2,000 course before they could work for him. Tony did not have that kind of money. So, at 17 years of age, he went to bank after bank until he found a banker who would loan him the $2,000 to get started. Then he talked about sleeping in his car at the 7-11 parking lot at night because he could not afford a place to stay.

THAT'S DRIVE.

Who among us is willing to work that hard?

I mentioned his other key: "Expect to succeed." Standing in front of the mirror, giving yourself positive affirmations will not work if deep down inside you don't believe it. I have no secret answer to this except, as I mentioned before:

> *Fill your mind with positive success-oriented material, books, tapes, live seminars—anything you can get your hands on. Then allow your mind to know that if all these successful people are saying the same thing they can not all be wrong. If you can allow your mind to be at least neutral when you take all this in, then after a while, it will start to sink in and you will begin to believe it.*

Tony Robbins has one complete tape on "Belief" and Wayne Dyer has a series entitled "You Will See It, When You Believe It." When your subconscious begins to believe it, your life will change.

Network marketing seems to have more than its fair share of obstacles for us to overcome. But the fact remains, some are successful and some are not. The successful network marketer has the same obstacles that everyone else has. I talk with some of the very successful front-line people in Changes every week or two. I can tell you THEY WORK HARD to earn the money they have. They don't give up easily and they always EXPECT to get through any temporary crisis we are having.

Please get your hands on as much success/motivational material you can and fill your mind with it. What you believe really makes a difference in your own personal success with Changes or anything. It really does! Take it from those who are successful. They know what they are talking about!

Now, to the specific obstacles in Changes.

We have had massive delays in getting the colloidal vitamins and minerals. This is because the formula for this product was not correct and would not stay in suspension. As a result, the manufacturing facility (before Twin Labs) took several weeks to reformulate the product and then a few more weeks to start cranking it out and get it to Changes. As a result, the company did not have any of the new product all of October and finally got a shipment in on November 13th. They are now working two shifts to get the product out to us.

The company now has an additional supplier and that should be kicking in the first of December. Also, the shipping and receiving building is now finished and we should be completely moved in by December. They have already been training additional personnel to work two shifts as soon as they get moved in. Yes, there is a backlog. But that should be taken care of quickly, as soon as we get moved in.

Scott has also hired additional management staff to help things run smoother in the future.

It is important at times like these to keep priorities straight. Sure, it is very frustrating to have these things happen to us. But even the best businesses and most successful people have things like this happen to them. Tony Robbins found out that one of his chief and most trusted individuals had embezzled three-quarters of a million dollars from him. How would you like that to happen to you? He was advised by all his advisors that bankruptcy was the only way out. But to them. He found a way to work through it. It was not easy, but he did it.

Now, we can all get angry and very frustrated because we have had a seeming rash of problems with Changes recently. Many have taken their hurt feelings and have gone somewhere else. But what is important? Your hurt feelings and frustration, or the potential money you can make? You can go to some other network marketing companies and get your product in a week and have phone calls answered on the first ring, but you will not make near the money you can make with Changes. We have proven this over and over.

So if your frustration and your feelings are more important than the money you earn with Changes, then that is your decision. Think of the frustration that any company president has to deal with. That is the nature of the business. But do they take their marbles and go home? No! They keep on working until they find a way through it.

Can you guess what company just reached a new high in the stock market and is recommended by some financial advisors? HERBALIFE!!

Can you imagine what those former distributors are thinking today who had a great income from Herbalife, but dropped out years ago when the company had its problems? I bet they get up every morning and kick themselves in their back side for the worst decision they ever made and the money that they would have these days if they had hung in there through the problems. Let's hope none of us will be doing the same thing a few years from now.

For anyone who does not know, I have a new 11-minute tape that I've been getting some good feedback on called "FACTS THAT NETWORK

MARKETING COMPANIES DON'T WANT YOU TO KNOW." There are loads of new tapes coming out and they all hype the products. Present and future network marketers need to know that you can have the hottest product in the world, but if the pay plan is weak, you will not make that "real MLM money" you can earn with a pay plan like Changes.

If you can afford to, send this tape back to anyone who sends you the latest, hot tape. If you cannot do this, then listen to it to take down the facts and send a transcript in a neatly typeset form.

I do appreciate the hard work everyone is putting in and I sincerely hope and truly BELIEVE that you will be greatly rewarded next year for the temporary frustration we have all experienced recently

If we are emotionally excited about the money potential/reality we have with Changes, we will automatically transfer that to anyone we talk with and that in turn will lead to more success. Be EXCITED! Excitement is contagious! Let's infect everyone.

❖ ❖ ❖

December 21, 1996
It is no big secret that Changes has had our supply and phone problems. Several other network marketing companies have sprung up copying our pay plan and offering better service. This is really interesting because for the first year of Changes, all the critics said our pay plan would never work and Changes would be out of business in no time. Funny how things change.

From the beginning I have always provided statistics and facts to show why Changes was better than other network marketing companies. Now I will do more of the same.

Although these numbers vary a bit, we know that something like 90 percent of all network marketing companies never last two years. We also know that those that do have a very high percentage of lasting five years or more. If you are thinking about jumping ship I hope you will consider these numbers carefully.

Every network marketing company that has been around for a while has experienced growth problems. This is the nature of the business. MBAs, accountants, and number–crunchers in mainstream business will all tell you that it is almost impossible for a company to sustain a 25-30 percent monthly growth rate and survive, yet Changes has done it. Instead of focusing on the problems we have had, think about how good the management must be to survive against those odds. Not only have we survived, we have survived EXTREMELY WELL! Do you know of any other network marketing company in history that after two and a half years in business still has 75 percent of all the distributors they have had? Never!

Does anyone who has jumped ship or is thinking about it really believe that these new companies will not have any problems? Some of the things these companies are promising have already been tried by Changes and Scotty and Terry know from experience that it will not work.

Here is more to consider. Scotty is getting a list of "former distributors" every day who are requesting to get back in. They left thinking that other fields looked greener and found out very quickly when they were there for a few months that all was not as it seemed. This is the "theory" of network marketing versus the "facts" that I have pushed about Changes from the very beginning.

❖   ❖   ❖

January 22, 1997

This will basically be a review of the meeting held here [in California] last weekend with Scott and Terry.

First, the meeting was very positive and Scott did not try and dodge any questions. He admitted that Changes has been through some rough times and was very well aware of the shipping delays and the clogged-up phone lines. Now everyone should be able to get through on the order lines within seconds and product is ready to go out the door within two hours of receiving the order.

Along this line, Scott mentioned again that in his listening trips through the customer service area, the vast majority of calls that are coming in are questions that should be answered by their sponsor or the Changes manual. He requested again, that for the sake of everyone involved with Changes, if you have a question, go to your sponsor first, then your next two upline and then consult the Changes manual. If these sources are not able to answer your questions, then call the company. The more people that use the customer line as a last resort, the less people will be trying to get through, which means it'll be easier to get through when it's really important.

He also stated that although the sales for November and December were down (which can be expected because of the Christmas season) the sales for January if continued at the same pace will DOUBLE that of December!

With regards to the new "competition" companies that have recently sprung up, they are playing off our supply problems of November and December, which are now a non-issue. Several people in the audience mentioned that they received product within one week of ordering from here in California. He also mentioned that he is receiving approximately 100 applications a day from former distributors wanting to get back into Changes.

I want to stick in here that if the "competitor" companies contact you or your downline to come right back with the statistics. 85 percent to 90 percent of all new companies do not last two years. Those who do last more than two years have an excellent chance of going on for another 5 to 10.

Who in their right mind would want to go against these percentages when you already have an established company, paying to most and now getting our supplies out on time? In addition to this, who says the other company will not have the same problems Changes had if they grow? I for one doubt it.

January, February and March are the three biggest diet months, so now is the time to push the Thermolift. Many people who have extra pounds to shed are thinking about losing weight even if they are not talking about it.

As far as the FDA trying to get ma huang [a Chinese herb used in some Changes product] off the market, that is a full-strength version. This is what is causing the problems. Our version is a standardized 8 percent solution, which is much less concentrated than what the FDA is talking about, and ours is considered completely safe. Our product contains 50 percent of what the law allows.

That is most of the material from the meeting. I will end with one marketing idea. See if you can get a list from your local Chamber of Commerce of all the small businesses in your town or area. Write a letter or send the "Dear Professional" letter and tell them about the Changes opportunity.

Small business owners are capable, self- motivated individuals. If you can get a few of these types of people, they are a higher caliber prospect than the average name from a mailing list. I would like to do it myself but I am on the phone most of the time with Changes distributors calling me. Someone should do what I suggest. If you do, please let me know.

❖   ❖   ❖

February 20, 1997
The tough times for Changes are history and we are blasting on into the future. The news just keeps getting better and better. Some of this is in the February *Changes Newsletter*. If you have not received it yet, it will come with your product order.

In spite of all the big full-page ads our new competitors have been running, January was up 30 percent over December. We reactivated 2,200 former distributors and enrolled 6,500 new ones. Changes has sent out 3,445 new distributor kits in the first 12 days of February. This represents a combination of reactivated and new distributors.

The new "impersonator" companies have not made a dent in the rapidly growing Changes membership. As of the end of January, we have 108,000 distributors and we are adding an average of 275 per day!

Some of the other competitors have already changed their pay plan and other items that they were using as promises to recruit Changes distributors. Those with good downlines who left to try one of the new companies are coming back, realizing the mistake they made. They now know where their *real* financial future is.

If you know any of these "lost sheep" who have realized the error of their ways, Changes will welcome them back with open arms. There are only a few "big name" people who have visibly made detracting comments about Changes, who will not be allowed to come back.

Another distributor is having great success recruiting new people simply using the Thermolift brochure and a sample pack stapled to it. He leaves these at restaurants when he goes out to eat or simply passes them out when he has a chance. When they buy a bottle of Thermolift, he shows them the advantages of becoming a distributor and then gives them more material on Changes. He is not encouraging these new people to get into the mail order end; his purpose, which is working well, is to isolate them from the onslaught of counter-offers by mail and phone that you get when you work by mail. He is building up another separate downline totally by word of mouth. I think this is a great idea for anyone willing to work this way.

I strongly encourage everyone to get Richard Poe's books on network marketing. They are filled with inspirational stories of people who failed several times in network marketing before they succeeded. These books are filled with great ideas on how to build your business.

There are only 108,000 distributors in Changes and there are estimates of 12 to 15 million network marketers. That means there are millions of people who are working an old-fashioned pay plan and have no idea what they are missing by not being involved with Changes. There are plenty of new prospects out there. All we need to do is go after them.

Mark Yarnell, in his beginning days with NuSkin, would go out between 8:00 and 10:00 AM and again between 4:00 and 6:00 PM, handing out his business card, talking with people on their way to work in the morning and on their way home at night. He worked it as a business. He worked hard. And look at what he accomplished! I am sure that anyone willing to do this would start building his or her downline very fast.

If you have not read Richard Poe's books, please go to your local bookstore and get them today. I guarantee they will get you motivated and give you lots of new ideas on how to build your business.

Thanks to everyone who stuck with Changes through the hard times. It is becoming very apparent that you made the right decision. My check for January was the largest ever. Yours should jump up also and if not, it will soon, the way the company is growing.

❖ ❖ ❖

March/April 1997
Each month, when it comes time to write this newsletter, if I don't have something specific to say I spend some time reading network marketing books and listening to tapes, looking for ideas that I consider valuable. In reviewing this material this time I came up to some conclusions.

1. Most of these supposed "network marketing experts" spend a lot of time talking about principles. Principles are good and necessary but that is not what makes your downline grow. You must have something to **do**. I mean ***physically do***.

2. Most of the rest who do give you things to do are things that the average person does not *want* to do, such as: approaching people, calling on the phone, giving meetings etc. Although I agree that these things do work, the simple fact is most people do not want to do this stuff. All the training and motivation you give someone is not going to get them to approach, call or sell people if that is not a part of their natural personality.

This is the reason I created the Changes three-step-system. I do not want to approach people in any way. I will not do this. It is simply not a part of my personality.

To this day I have never approached any of my friends, relatives or strangers about Changes. I have done it all by mail. Yes, I have spent a lot of time talking to people, but only when they called me or asked me to return their call.

So what I would like to review is things that you can DO or you can give your downline or new prospects to do. These are things that will not contradict the introverted personality such as mine. These are not new, but they are actual physical things that you or your downline can do to build your business.

1. Mail postcards, flyers or the booklet *Secrets of Network Marketing Plans Revealed.*

2. Advertise in network marketing publications such as *Cutting Edge, Money & Profits, Network Trainer, Network Opportunities,* or *Success.* We need network marketing *workers.*

3. Advertise in your local newspapers for "Professionals or Business Owners."

4. Buy mailing lists of network marketers, business owners or professionals.

5. Get on as many lists as you can and mail back to these people.

Here is a principle to keep in mind. MASSIVE EFFORT EQUALS MASSIVE RESULTS.

No one is going to get rich mailing out 25 postcards a week. You have got to do more. I never recommend going over your budget, but I do recommend spending as much as you can possibly afford in promoting your business.

For the past few months I have not been advertising Changes. First, my health has not been the best, and secondly I was getting complaints that I was taking all the good advertising. But now all I see is big, full-color ads by some of our copy-cat competitors and virtually no ads for Changes. So if you are not going to advertise Changes, I certainly will. This is one of the main ways I built my business—ADVERTISING TO NETWORK MARKETERS. Showing them with all kinds of facts and statistics that Changes is absolutely, positively the best thing going.

There is no way an introvert like myself or many of my other key distributors could have made the kind of money we are making in any other network marketing company.

I got a call last week from a lady who is very big in one of the phone companies and was coming over to Changes. Although she had been very successful in this company before they changed the pay plan, she had never even heard of working network marketing by mail. It was a totally new concept. She was amazed at the money we are making without ever giving meetings.

The point to this is that there are millions of network marketers out there who are working their buns off for peanuts and have no awareness of a pay plan like Changes or working network marketing by mail. In your daily contact with friends or business associates if anyone even mentions they know someone is working "one of those MLM or pyramid programs" then GET THEIR NAME AND ADDRESS IMMEDIATELY and mail them a booklet. Open their eyes.

Sometimes the excitement may wane off, but the way we make money is to keep on working and building your business. Just because we don't have to punch a clock with Changes does not mean we can take it too easy—that is if you want that residual income check to grow. I'm not stopping.

If you are working Changes by mail or advertising and do not want to answer the phone 24 hours a day, there is a new service that allows you to advertise an 800 number, have a live operator answer the phone 24 hours a day and then fax you the leads. What a great idea. I will be using this. This service will add to the duplication of our system.

Thank you for your continued work.

❖ ❖ ❖

June, 1997
Changes has the highest payout in the industry. If any other company claims otherwise, let them provide an audited statement from a respectable CPA firm. Have no worry, no one will do this. But you will probably hear lots of excuses.

With regard to our two new products, think how many people would like to lose weight but have not wanted a ma huang product. Now we have one. Think of the people who suffer from joint pain. We now have a totally natural product for them. We now automatically have thousands and thousands of new prospects and potential distributors. Every time Changes comes out with new products our checks go up.

❖ ❖ ❖

July, 1997
This month's newsletter will basically be a summary of the recent Changes meeting in California. There are some very interesting developments that everyone

should know about, including the fact that Changes is on track for $50 million in sales this year.

We had the 7th largest accounting firm in the world do a complete audit for the last two years. It is now totally certified that we payout an average of 61 percent—the highest in the industry. (One major network marketing company compares at 43 percent.)

Terry & Scott are running full–page ads in all of the top trade publications. People who call the advertised 800 number will be given out on a rotational basis to a list of three and four star execs.

Sales tax. We're getting big enough, so we're going to have to start keeping track of it. To get out of paying it on your personal consumption, keep track of how much you don't sell or give away, because you'll be able to get the sales tax back at the end of the year.

A new detailed training manual is being developed. In the future, company newsletters will be set up in a way so that new materials can be added easily. We will have samples of all of the products.

Self-manufacturing. This would save an additional 14 percent in costs. Some of this will go into incentive programs such as awards, trips, and possibly a car bonus. This is a ways off and please be assured that commission scales will never be touched in setting up a bonus system. Reasons for self–manufacturing: complete control over product development, quality, etc.

Benefits of the new phone & computer system. Personalized Pin numbers, different from your Social Security. 800 number for customers. They'll use your ID number and the company will collect money, ship and pay you the retail profit from the sale. Three-way calling to allow you the ability to settle matters directly with the company and whoever is having problems. Touch-tone, 24-hour ordering system. 800 numbers for group broadcasting of important messages. Access to your genealogy over the phone. Immediate order processing with the new computer setup.

A new West Coast shipping center and eventually several more around the country, which will greatly speed up shipments. All orders are being processed within 24 hours, so the times it takes to get you is just travel time.

A new Changes Credit Card. Credit based on your monthly Changes income. Delinquencies will be paid straight out of your Changes earnings. Hopefully, it will be set up so that no one will be turned down. Merchant accounts so you can accept credit card orders from customers.

They're adding a medical advisory board and much more support info on the products. A voice mail system will give product info and let you leave a message with additional questions.

An extensive survey on our industry by the DSA is being used to help create new marketing strategies. For example, the personal care industry is three times the size of the vitamin industry, so at some point they will ad a personal care line.

Work is being done to set up in other countries. All materials will be available in Spanish & English.

The company is continually create new marketing strategies and materials so we will all have lots of ways to expand our business. Knowledge is power and we want to be the best-trained sales force in network marketing.

Again, thank you to everyone for your continuing efforts. The new developments coming our way are sure to continue to make Changes the best opportunity in Network Marketing.

❖   ❖   ❖

August, 1997
I just returned from my summer vacation. In addition to spending some valuable time in nature, I spent a lot of time reading success stories of some of our modern day business leaders. We can learn from their successes and apply the lessons to our Changes business.

Most of these individuals have qualities you will read about in success-oriented material but I would like to focus on a few of the qualities that are not so common. Here are some qualities that stood out to me.

1. They did things or accomplished things that "others" said could not be done. No matter how the odds were stacked against them, they kept thinking and rethinking the problem until their creativity came up with an answer. This is the mental version of not giving up. They kept rehashing the situation over and over again in their minds until they finally came up with an answer.

2. They were not afraid to break the rules. Many times these entrepreneurs came up with a solution to the problem that was so different that everyone else said "you can't do *that*. It isn't done that way. You will be considered an oddball if you try." But they kept their own belief and went ahead and did it any way and became successful.

3. You have heard it said: "Work smart, not hard." These leaders worked both smart and hard. Many worked fourteen and sixteen hours a day, but they enjoyed the work. They had a passion for what they were doing. In a way it was not work for them, but fun.

4. They accept their dream or their version of something that was very possible and even probable for them to attain. They were not limited

by what many would call handicaps of youth, starting capital, no MBA or business training or anything else. When Bill Gates came up with a bold idea of writing a computer language that all computers of the future could use, he did not think "hey, I'm just a punk kid college drop out." Instead he said, "I can do this." And he did.

5. For many situations that people would consider PROBLEMS, these successful people approached as delightful CHALLENGES. It is as if, in their minds they were saying: "You think you can stop me or beat me, I'll show you. Get ready, because here I come."

As we continue to build our Changes business, let's keep these leadership qualities in mind. When we have a problem or something that may seem to be a setback, let's review these qualities and apply them to our own situation.

Summer is usually a slow time for network marketing because it is a time for summer vacations and many are away from home. In spite of this, Changes has continued to grow and add new distributors.

Now as September and the Fall season approaches, it is the perfect time to renew our efforts to build our businesses and our income. It is the best time to do more of what we have already been doing or, *even better*, try different or unique approaches. Many are still having success handing out our Thermolift samples with their name and phone number attached.

I plan to remail a letter or something new to all leads that came in over summer but did not join. If you know or hear of anyone who is working another network marketing company you must either get my *Secrets* booklet or the company booklet "In the World of Network Marketing, All Companies are not Created Equal." There are thousands of network marketers working so hard to build their business and they have no idea what they could be earning. Either of these booklets will get them informed.

Here is an idea:

"Want to lose weight but don't want the side effects of ma huang? Lose weight naturally without getting wired."

I thank you again for your continued hard work and dedication. We are making history in network marketing.

❖   ❖   ❖

September 1997
One of the main reasons people get into network marketing is to get that residual income, that nice check coming in month after month with little or no work. This is what CHANGES offers that very few other companies offer to the majority of their distributors.

A professional network marketer can build a big downline and earn a nice check in just about any company. But because the average person does not make money they soon drop out and it is a continual recruiting process to keep that money coming in. You probably know of one big name player for another company who continually travels around the country giving big recruiting seminars to keep his check going.

I personally know of another professional network marketer who is a very helpful, hard-working and ethical person. But he continually joins companies that have big breakaway pay plans. He earns big checks for a while, then when all the average people he has recruited do not earn a profit, they start dropping out. He has to start all over again.

As many of you know, I have not been feeling well for the past several months and I have been able to give very little time to the downline I built or continue building. But my checks have stayed within a very narrow range and I just received the largest check ever.

Here is the point of all this. When you are talking to a prospect about Changes be sure and stress the STAYING POWER & CONTINUAL RESIDUAL INCOME the Changes pay plan offers, like no other company. We have all been promoting the fact that with the Changes pay plan a new person can get into profit quickly and that is what leads to success. As we all know, this is absolutely the case. But now is the time to push the other powerful aspect of this pay plan, which is the ABSOLUTELY AMAZING STAYING POWER IT PROVIDES.

It is like the Eveready bunny—it just keeps on paying and paying and paying. Your downline does not evaporate or disappear.

One of the most frequent requests is for past issues of my downline letters. We have now compiled many of these and are making them available to anyone who wants them. We are calling it *The Best of Joe's Downline Letters*. Some of the information in the early letters is out of date, but it gives a good idea of how I learned and how ideas shifted along the way. But most of all there is a wealth of marketing info packed into these letters. This is the first time they have all been available at once. If you would like one, send $10 check or money order and it will go out right away.

I am enclosing some copies of a few pages from a network marketing magazine. It is good information and I just wanted to pass it along. I have no affiliation with them. If you want to order, it looks pretty good.

I am also enclosing a new "bounce back" letter that seems to be pulling well. I mail this back to people who send me network marketing offers in the mail. So far I am getting one to three of these sent back to me each day wanting more information. Feel free to copy it and try it yourself.

I keep seeing more and more copy cat network marketing companies in various publications. When Scott and Terry first came out with the 15 percent, 45 percent and 15 percent everybody said it would not work. Now everyone and his brother is jumping on the bandwagon with an exact duplicate or very similar marketing plan. They have seen the success of Changes and they know it is the best plan going. Changes is the first, it is the best and we are in a great situation being with this company at this time.

October and November are two really good months for network marketing. Let's give it all we've got so we can have the most prosperous Christmas ever.

I sincerely appreciate everyone's continued work.

❖   ❖   ❖

October, 1997
WOW! WOW! WOW!

We have the greatest pay plan that pays out the most to its members. No one has responded to our 61 percent challenge. You know why? Because they can't. So they try to bamboozle innocent prospects with claims beyond claims and glitzy ads. They know they cannot compete when they have to talk about FACTS.

Just a quick remark about an article in the latest issue of *Network Opportunities*. It is called "Two Level Pay Plans—Do They Work?" While the article was well-written and provided a relatively good analysis, it missed the whole point. It states that this type of pay plan has not attracted any big heavy-hitters and probably will not.

THIS IS ABSOLUTELY RIGHT! Changes takes the enormous amounts that would normally go to a heavy-hitter and spreads it out among everyone else. That is the whole reason Scotty and Terry created this type of pay plan. How could someone write a basically good review of our pay plan and MISS THE ENTIRE POINT? Well maybe he did not "miss the point." He just did not want people to know. Then they would call his number at the end of the article and be sold on his "heavy hitter-potential-payout" program. To bad for them—huh?

Please pass this letter to your downline and encourage everyone to join the "Incite" program.

Will I make more money? Yes. But so will you. It automatically helps everyone.

Thanks again to Scotty and Terry Paulsen for once again coming up with an ingenious idea, an idea that will put more money in the pockets of all of us.

❖   ❖   ❖

November, 1997
The good news from Changes seems to never stop. What a difference from this time last year when we were experiencing severe product delays, mix-ups and a lot of disgruntled customers and distributors.

For everyone who has stuck with Changes and continued to work it has really paid off. This merger with TWIN LABS for all practical purposes has turned Changes into the golden goose. And we get to pick up the golden eggs.

Lets go over just what this means to us.

1. SECURITY, SECURITY AND MORE SECURITY! What is the #1 worry for any network marketing distributor? Their company is here today and gone tomorrow. Now that we have merged with one of the

largest nutritional companies in the world we can be sure this will never happen. They have tremendous financial assets to make sure Changes not only sticks around but continues to grow. Friends, this is a dream come true. We have got to be the envy of every network marketing company out there. This is really big, GREAT NEWS. It is hard to exaggerate what this means for us.

2. OUR OWN MANUFACTURING FACILITY—MANY MORE PRODUCTS.
The more we have to sell, the larger our check will be. Here is a great example. I can not mention any names, but a well-known network marketing company built its entire business based on an audio tape. Several months ago they stopped using the tapes. But the company has continued to grow at a very good pace. How were they able to do this? When they stopped using the tape they added several new products. So the distributors already had a good customer base, all they had to do was sell them more products. And they did. Now that we will have more products we can do the same.

3. NAME RECOGNITION.
Who outside of the network marketing world has heard of Changes? Not many. But anyone who is at the very least familiar with nutrition and especially the fitness and body building industry is very familiar with TWIN LABS. They are in every health food store and nutritional center around. They are a Big, Big name. This name recognition builds **safety** and **TRUST** for new prospects considering trying our products. So when you approach a new customer you can say, "Our company is Changes, we are a division of TWIN LABS, one of the most well known and respected nutritional companies in the world."

I already have word that when this news came out, at least one big player in another network marketing company brought his entire downline over. So if you know of anyone in another company who may have been sitting on the fence regarding Changes, now is the time to give that person a call. Remember, this merger with TWIN LABS is the closest thing any network marketer is ever going to get to ultimate security. Changes is going to be around for a long, long time.

I am not sure at this point if we can use the name TWIN LABS in any advertising or mailing, but we can sure mention it to others. Changes will be running full page ads in the major network marketing publications announcing this news. This will give us as a company and distributors the respect we deserve.

It is said that December is a hard time to build a network marketing business because everyone is budgeting their money for Christmas presents. But if you ever get this as an "excuse" for not trying our products, we can come back with: "Wouldn't it be nice if you could afford a much larger Christmas next year? Now is the time to start. Not later. Most of the time, later never happens."

Very few network marketing companies ever last five years. We are rapidly approaching that three year birthday. With this merger this is almost guaranteed. Now it is time to take our hats off, take a bow and give ourselves a pat on the back. We have accomplished what very few have done plus we are making great money in the process.

HOW ABOUT THAT!

❖   ❖   ❖

February, 1998
It seems that everybody today is running ads and mailing you postcards saying that they have a "system" and that they will do all the work for you.

I think we can compete with this, to some degree, by at least promoting that we have a system. Now we have all the tools. It is just a matter of promoting it as a system. You can make up your own, but for example:

THIS SYSTEM HAS BUILT ONE OF THE MOST SUCCESSFUL NETWORK MARKETING COMPANIES TODAY WITH AN UNUSUALLY HIGH DISTRIBUTOR RETENTION RATE!

Step 1. Call this two-minute recorded message [my number].

Step 2. Call or write the person who sent you this card and have them send you our booklet *Secrets of Network Marketing Revealed.*

Step 3. Sign up and mail this same postcard.

You can make up your own, but the idea is to promote what you are doing as a "system" that is working.

Mailing lists. The problem we have with most mailing lists in my opinion is getting a lot of people who like the idea of making money from their home, but they do not want to work. I am enclosing mailing list rates from *Success* magazine. Or try Conant/Nightingale. These people are usually much more success- oriented and should be hard workers.

What to say in our new advertising?

One distributor is having great success running very simple ads regarding the price of our products as compared with most network marketing companies. I don't think it would be fair to give you word for word what is working but it seems that there are a lot of network marketers out there who are unsatisfied with the price they are paying for their products.

The new products come out this month, so I think we can all look for an increase in our checks. The more products we have, the more we should be able to sell.

Every month I hear about more and more network marketers with large groups coming over to Changes. Why? The word is out. While their checks keep going down, the checks of Changes distributors keep going up. The secret word is "residual income."

P.S. You can order the names from *Success* magazine on your own if you choose. Or since the minimum order is 5,000 names, if I can get four other distributors to go in with me, I will order the names and divvy them out. With peel and stick labels, it looks like this will be about $120 each. Call me if you are interested.

Watch for the following information in upcoming newsletters from Changes. Sample packs on five Changes products, expanded, revised and improved distributor kit, two new audio tapes, a new List Distribution # system so you will not have to use your Social Security number, auto-ship and a new company video.

❖ ❖ ❖

March/April 1998 Newsletter
I have been working on an 800 toll–free recruiting system for my downline. I have already gotten approval for the opening three–minute message. At that point the new prospect is encouraged to either leave their name and address and phone so that a distributor can get back to them or access another system of phone mail boxes where they can hear such things as:

How My System Evolved

1. The benefit of this automatic recruiting system.
2. Facts on Changes including the fact that we have a VERY HIGH percentage of distributors achieving success compared to other companies.
3. Pay plan comparison and why comparing only the first three of four levels is misleading.
4. Product testimonials.
5. Income testimonials.
6. Product descriptions.
7. Fax on demand.
8. *Secrets of Network Marketing Plans Revealed* by fax and maybe more.

CAUTION-WARNING This last part is not approved yet and is not by any means final. I am just sharing the ideas I am working with and asking for **comments or suggestions on how we can make this more "turn-key" and successful**.

So please fax me your ideas or comments.

Regarding advertising or promotion. There has been a change in policy regarding this from Changes. We no longer have to get promotional materials approved as long as they are "blind ads." This means you can not use the names "Changes," "Twin Labs" or mention any of the products by name. (Descriptions are okay.) This is great news, but let's not get carried away. Wild claims and statements hurt not only you and other Changes distributors but damage the reputation of the company. So use this good news with wisdom and care in building your business. If you have any doubts you may still want to run it by the home office for clearance, but this does take time.

I am also considering running some generic TV advertisements for people who are looking for home-based businesses. I will probably try this myself first to try to determine the quality of responses we will be getting. If I get 500 responses and they are all "tire-kickers" then obviously this is not what we want.

It is common knowledge in marketing that your present customer list is absolutely the best people to market to. Here is how we can use this fact to our advantage. Even though we have one of the highest percentages of distributors being successful, we do have inactive members. They were interested in Changes at one time but for many and various reasons they have become inactive. In the past three or four months there have been many positive changes to the company including the merger with Twin Labs, all the new products and the new computer system. What Scotty is encouraging all the leaders to do is write a letter to these inactive distributors telling them about all the positive changes that have happened.

Here it is how it can work: you can call the company and find out how many inactive distributors you have in your downline. This can be a total (for example) of your first three, five or ten levels. Once you have decided how many of these distributors you want to mail to, if we print the letters, put the postage on the envelopes and put them in the box and send them to Changes. They will apply the appropriate address labels to your letter and mail them out.

The idea is for an inactive distributor to receive the letter from their sponsor and several levels in their upline. This barrage of letters should cause enough excitement to bring a large portion of these people in. This should be timed so that they go out around the last of April or the first few weeks of May. Thus when a former distributor calls in to the company they will be impressed by the new computer system that will be in place by then. They will see that we are growing not only in numbers of distributors, but growing with the technology age.

There may or may not be a copy of my letter along with this newsletter. You can use this as an example for ideas but do not copy it word for word. Each letter from someone in their upline should be different.

Now that I'm past some health problems, I plan to put my creative energies to work not only in mail and phone systems but also the "possibility" of traveling to meetings and conference calls, if I can think of anything to say. I am open for suggestions along this line. I hope there is enough good news in this letter to get all of us encouraged to build this wonderful residual income we have with this great company even further. It is because of your continued work that I am able to say in person and in print "I was unable to work for some time and my check just keeps on coming month after month."

That is an amazing statement with regard to network marketing. This is the dream of everyone getting in to network marketing, yet so few actually achieve it. I am able to make this statement because of the Changes amazing pay plan and your continued work and dedication through the good times and bad.

❖ ❖ ❖

Inactive Distributor Letter

After Changes International merged with the major nutritional supplement company Twin Labs in October of 1997, I sent a short letter out to anyone who had ever explored the Changes opportunity with me. Here's what I mailed out:

❖ ❖ ❖

Dear Changes Distributor:

There are many reasons why a distributor may choose to become inactive. I am sure yours are legitimate and valid. However, as your upline in Changes I wanted to let you know about some tremendous improvements that have happened to our company in the past few months. It is my hope than when you fully realize the scope of these improvements and how they affect you as a user of our products and as a part-time business opportunity, you may reconsider.

First, in October of last year Changes International merged with Twin Labs. Twin Labs is one of the major nutritional supplement companies in the world. They have maintained an excellent reputation for years and are a Fortune 500 company traded in the New York Stock Exchange.

This merger gives us tremendous credibility. From now on, when asked who makes our products, the answer is Changes International, a division of Twin Labs. Rather than "Changes who?" this name recognition makes it significantly easier for a new prospect to take a chance or try one of our products. Now we have real "status."

For us business builders, those who work Changes as a source of income, this is the best news we could ever possibly hope to have.

Why?

As you probably very well know, most network marketing companies do not last two years. We have all heard story after sad story of someone who had spent months and sometimes years building a profitable downline only to have the company go under. This is one of the main drawbacks of network marketing—not knowing how long your company is going to last.

How My System Evolved

Now that Changes is part of a tremendous financial power house like Twin Labs, the chances of this happening to us are extremely remote. This merger gives long term financial stability. As far as you are concerned, this means if you have built a business and an income with Changes, as long as you continue to work your business, that paycheck will continue to come month after month, year after year. This is the dream of multi-level marketing. Now we have achieved it.

This merger has enabled us to make a much larger variety of products available to you and your downline. When Changes first started out we had two products. Now we have twenty. Here are some of our latest additions:

New products. *Time-Fighters Anti-Aging Multi-Formula For Women With Iron, Time-Fighters Anti-Aging Multi-Formula For Women Without Iron, Time-Fighters Anti-Aging Multi-Formula For Men, Best Friends Multi-Formula For Kids, Sharp Thinking Mental Alertness Formula, Brighten Up Herbal Mood Elevator, Good Night for a Restful Nights Sleep, Soy Defense— Protective Phytonutrients For Men & Women from the Miracle Soybean,* plus all of the wonderful Changes products you are already familiar with.

In May, we will have a new, sophisticated computer system. This will allow us to have a totally automated ordering system and will enable any distributor to have access to his or her downline at a moment's notice.

Soon we will have the auto-order option back, which can insure you will never miss a paycheck because you may have been too busy and forgot to order this month. We have hired a programmer who for years worked with one of the major network marketing companies of the world.

In other words, we have moved quickly into the technology age. We are a force to be reckoned with.

It is possible that one reason you may have become inactive is because you were talked into getting involved in another network marketing company. I know that almost every company out there is now claiming to have "the best pay plan ever." It is easy to make a claim. It is also easy to talk about potential payout and do tricks with numbers.

But here is what you need to consider: Changes International has one of the highest percentages of distributors sticking with it and staying active that we know of. And the reason we have to say "we know of" is because most network marketing companies will not tell you their activity rate. Why? Probably because they are embarrassed and don't want anyone to know.

What does this mean for you?

It means that on a strictly mathematical basis you have a better chance of succeeding with us than most. Any mathematician will tell you it is always better to go with the odds rather than against them.

Don't be fooled by empty claims or a fast talker on the other end of the phone. In most network marketing companies, most people fail. With Changes many succeed. Please think about this.

If for some reason you left because you did not get along with your sponsor, you can chose to come back in under another sponsor once you have been inactive for three months. Please don't let a former disagreement or misunderstanding keep you from enjoying our fabulous products and the best opportunity we know of to earn a nice income from the comfort of your home.

We would love to have you back. Please consider all of the above when making your decision. You can get in touch with your sponsor if you have their name or phone number or you can contact someone in your upline, me, or the company itself.

We'd love to hear from you.

❖   ❖   ❖

We didn't get everyone back, but the letter was effective. It was full of positive good news and reassuring information that replaced negative memories and impressions. Time might heal all wounds and wound all heels, but don't count on distributors drifting back to your business after they have forgiven and forgot. Out of sight, out of mind is a better rule to remember.

❖   ❖   ❖   ❖   ❖

Summing Up My Secrets

You learn along the way, and that's known as experience. If you're willing to take a risk, you'll generally have a broader range of experience, and have more of a chance for success. One of the ways I built my business was going after other network marketers. This was in direct opposition to the way which was normally promoted, which is finding customers new to network marketing. If you can find people who are already risk-takers, you are going to do a lot better. That's my philosophy, because the average person on the street is not a risk-taker. They are pretty much content with their job or whatever they are doing and are not really willing to risk their time or their money to better themselves. That's not a judgment on who they are, that's just the type of personality you usually find.

Traditional network marketing teaches you to promote to your family, your friends, your neighbors and co-workers, but even when I started making really huge checks, my friends and family were still not interested. They were never interested—even though I'm making more than all of them right now. I have always tried to do as much as I can to share everything I know about success, first in phone calls, then in my newsletters. My "success kit" is the priority mail envelope.

I spent years of learning and learned from my failures. You have to be willing to fail. I failed many times, but most all people who have succeeded have failed—particularly in network marketing. I know very few people who quit their job and became an overnight success in network marketing. They had to learn the ropes and that involved failing. No one is ever going to be a successful network marketer if they are afraid to fail. You fail, you figure out what you learn, you pull yourself up by your bootstraps, and you go on. There is no college education for this.

No one taught me the ropes; I discovered courses like this after I became a success. I never took a course on how to write sales letters or how to write ads. You just learn by practice; you try one time and you do it over and over, and through the years, you develop a knack for it.

My newsletters provide an historical perspective. At one time, we could use income testimonials, later we could not. You can see the problems we went through, but eventually Changes International merged with a highly-respected national nutritional company whose products are sold in grocery and drug stores across the country. Changes went from an idea based on experience to one of the great all-time success stories in multi-level marketing. Despite claims from "experts" who said the pay plan could not work, despite magazine reviews that slammed the company only to retract the statements later, despite troubles with product formulation and delivery, we managed to expand beyond my wildest initial expectations.

The basic secret to any successful network marketing company is a duplicatable system, in conjunction with a fair pay plan. Keeping your downline informed of new developments on a monthly basis and as often as necessary is a big part of taking care of your distributors, which is the other essential element of network marketing success. If your downline is happy, you'll keep them, and your business will continue to expand.

You probably noticed in the newsletters I shared with you that I occasionally mentioned sources of personal inspiration. No matter how perfect the system you use, whether you hold meetings or work through the mail like I did, if a distributor does not believe in the possibilities of their own success, nothing you can do will help. It's one thing to refine your system; it's just as important to refine your mind. That's why I'd like to share with you how I was able to convince myself that success was okay.

7
BRAINWASH YOURSELF FOR SUCCESS

In my "former life," when I was eking out a living taping lectures at the Whole Life Expo and other conventions, I often wondered how the successful people at the lectern were so self–assured. Whether they were talking about the benefits of wheat grass juice or how to find your soulmate, they all had something in common. They were all so positive!

Doesn't that just make you sick? Doesn't it seem like a sham when you see someone carrying on that way? I mean, aren't they trying to sell you something? Greed, greed, greed.

Doesn't it sound just like Michael Douglas' character Gordon Gekko in the movie "Wall Street." You know the scene, where he stands up before a group of stockholders and declares: "Greed. Greed is good!" Money, money, money, that's all people think about.

That's not true, but it describes a negative attitude I had, at least some of the time. It took me a while to get over it. There's nothing wrong with making a lot of money. Greed is something else entirely. I never got greedy, but when I learned what a great, positive difference money can make in a person's life, I changed my attitude entirely. I didn't just wake up one day with a different state of mind, though. I had to do a lot of study, which included learning how many others had been in circumstances much like mine before Changes International. Doing so helped me get over a great personal barrier, and realize that money is okay.

This was something I had to find out on my own, because being the head of a downline, people looked to me for answers. Remember what I said earlier. The way to network marketing success does not come by thinking "What can I do to get rich?" but "What can I do to help my downline?" The problem is, who helps the person at the top of a network marketing organization? When you're the person everyone is looking to for answers, where do you get them, if you don't have them?

People who spend a lot of time helping others quite often forget to help themselves. I know I did. When you get busy running a business, it's easy to ignore the one essential element of that business—the person at the core of it all. And why not? It's easy to see what others are doing, and not so easy to observe yourself. It's easy to skip a meal, go without sleep, thinking that you'll catch up later. Then when later catches up with you, it can often hit suddenly and with great devastation, as your body and your mind finally say "Enough already!" You have to remember to keep taking care of yourself, and that includes seeing after your own personal mental and physical health.

The Lincoln Example

Great success often comes after heart-breaking failure, which is another reason you need to stay as mentally and physically fit as possible. If you're healthy, it's easier to cope with setbacks. In my experience, it all begins in the mind. No matter how unique your circumstances seem, no matter how bleak your prospects look, someone has been there before, and many of them went on to great success. You can, too, but first you have to convince yourself that it's possible. You have to brainwash yourself into it, become so mentally surrounded by ideas of success that there is no room in your mind for anything but success. I found in reading about fantastically successful people that many of them failed many times before making it, and many failed after making it. Walt Disney, for example, went bankrupt three times.

Just as I had bailed out of a dozen network marketing companies yet continued to doggedly pursue my dream, so had many other people in their chosen careers. Take Abraham Lincoln. He had less than a year of formal education in his entire life. When he first ran for office in 1832, he was defeated, but two years later he ran again and was elected to the Illinois legislature. While in office, he studied for the bar and became a lawyer. He was elected to the U.S. Congress from the Seventh Congressional District of Illinois in 1846 but only served one term, as was the custom in his district at the time. In 1855, he became a candidate for the U.S. Senate but lost, just as he did the next go-around against Senator Stephen A. Douglas. When he won the Republican nomination for President in 1860, he might not have been elected if the Democratic party had not split into two factions, North and South, in addition to there being another party, the Constitutional Union Party.

Noteworthy success is never easily attained, even for the greatest people in our lives. I often talk to my downline about this. I continually encourage them to fill their minds with the stories of people who have succeeded. Whether you study historical perspectives, or read about new business successes in Forbes magazine, reading about successful people is very important. I also believe in listening to any type of success tape you can get your hands on. I am almost always listening to some sort of success or motivational information tape in my car, or whenever I get a chance. I've found that you can "brainwash yourself for success" by filing your mind with stories about successful people. You don't have to listen to many of them before you realize that successful people have failed many times, but don't give up easily. They are eternal optimists, and they keep on going despite the obstacles.

Are the Rich Really That Bad?

Back to the subject of money. Usually, money accompanies success. Not always, but it's usually true. I've found that people who don't have money have two things going against them, mentally:

1. they believe money is bad; or
2. they don't believe they deserve it.

You may have seen examples of (2) on television, when some movie or TV stars talk about their amazing good fortune. "Why me?" they'll ask. Or they'll say, "Sometimes I feel a little guilty about all this success." Of course, when we see them drive away from the interview in their new luxury car or chauffeur-driven limousine, we wonder just how guilty they really feel.

The media can leave you jaded about successful people, and the tabloids continually exploit celebrity failings, but that kind of thing drives TV ratings up and sells newspapers and magazines. The rich, successful people who do good works with their wealth don't get nearly the public notice.

My life was changed the first time Texas billionaire Ross Perot ran for President and his campaign committee began running television ads about all the positive things that he had done. I paid close attention to all the good things he did with his money. The simple fact is, when I saw all the good things he had done with his money, there was some sort of a flip in my mind. I realized, in an epiphany that sounds almost silly, that "Yes, you can do good with money."

You see, I grew up with a philosophy along the lines of: "We're poor folk, we'll always be poor folk, and the rich people got that way from stomping on everybody else." It was a pervasive attitude in my psyche, a subconscious point–of–view that blocked me from achieving success. On some hidden level, I equated money with the greed of bad, rich people. I also believed, probably due to years of failing, that somehow I did not deserve success.

So there I was, believing that money is bad and that even if I did come into a lot of money, I didn't deserve it, anyway.

Talk about self-defeating!

After I saw those Perot ads and began to think about all the good things I could do if I made a lot of money, things began to change. I thought about all the "gurus" I had seen speak at the Whole Life Expo and I began to soak up as much positive information as I could find. I embarked on a continuous pattern of positive "brainwashing" by reading books and listening to tapes. After a while, it began to make a big difference.

When I started realizing it was okay to make a lot of money and have a lot of money that I could use to do good things, my business started taking off and the amounts of my checks kept going up and up. If nothing else, I was helping a lot of people make more money than they had ever thought possible in a network marketing company, while distributing good products. That alone was worthwhile.

Poor self–image is a very common problem, even with people near the top of their profession. While campaigning for the nomination of his party in 1859, Abraham Lincoln doubted himself. In a letter to Thomas J. Pickett, the editor of the *Rock Island* (Illinois) *Register* newspaper, he wrote: "I must, in candor, say I do not think I am fit for the presidency."

History decided differently, but even Honest Abe had some personal problems to work through.

Profiles of Success

Every magazine will supply any potential advertiser with a data card for each quarter of any fiscal year. This card, whose claims are always certified by an independent body, describe in detail the statistic and demographics of the magazine's readership. If you're thinking about advertising with a magazine, ask to see their data card and make sure that the claims have been certified. If they have not, you may be dealing with information that is not reliable, and thus you shouldn't advertise with this publication.

The *Success* magazine data card for the first quarter of 1998 provides a very good profile of the type of person you might want to recruit into your downline. The magazine stated a circulation of almost half a million people, 58.3 percent men and 41.7 percent women. The median age listed was 38.7, while 85 percent of the readers were aged 25 to 54. College education was prominent, with 66.1 percent of the readers either attending or graduating. The net worth of the readers was $688,000 and the median household income was $115,540. The occupation that predominated was professional/managerial, with 63.5 percent of the readers.

If you think this type of person wouldn't be interested in network marketing, better think again. I hope you recall what I mentioned earlier about the doctor making $1,000,000 a year who got into network marketing with his wife and made even more.

Granted, you don't need a college degree to succeed in this business, and there's no college course I know of to teach you how to make it in network marketing, but one thing should be clear. Even though the readers of this magazine had mostly gone to college, they still continued to study and improve their zone of knowledge. In network marketing, this aspect alone can be all-important.

The Man Who Brought Network Marketing into the Mainstream

My own story of many failures before success is not at all unique in network marketing. That's one reason I recommend that my downline read books like *The Wave 3 Way to Building Your Downline* by Richard Poe. He has some very interesting ideas, like the Butterfly Effect, which basically states that the wind movements created by the beating wings of a single tiny butterfly can cause changes in air currents that can have a ripple effect impacting the entire atmosphere of the planet. (The point being that network marketers can often achieve massive personal results through minimal personal efforts.) But that's not the main reason I advise they read the book. Poe relates one inspiring story after another about people who have failed and then succeeded, who suffered through terrible hardships until finding the right network marketing company. Once they found success—which often looked like it would never come—they managed to pay off personal debts of half a million dollars. Can you imagine what most people would have done, facing a situation like that?

It takes positive people to succeed. Richard Poe is not only very positive, but the main writer responsible for bringing network marketing into the mainstream. In 1990, he wrote a column for *Success* magazine entitled "Network Marketing: The Most Powerful Way to Reach Consumers in the 90s." Anyone who has ever built a substantial business in network marketing has seen a copy of that article. It was wildly popular when it ran, and two years later *Success* ran "We Create Millionaires," the first positive cover story about network marketing. Because of Poe, *Success* was the first publication to talk about network marketing as a legitimate business as opposed to a "get rich quick" scheme, so our hats will always be off to him. Going against the conventional wisdom of his editors at *Success*, Poe stuck his neck out and stated his opinion. When I found out why he was so positive, and unafraid to do something he knew was right though not yet popular, I discovered we had been on similar paths.

The Father of Positive Mental Attitudes

One of the former editors of *Success* magazine was Napoleon Hill, who wrote a very famous book called *Think and Grow Rich* and later *Keys to Success*. If you're pre–disposed to think making money is bad, like I mentioned earlier, you probably never opened *Think and Grow Rich* even if you came across it. It sounds like "Wishing for Money" or something. That's not what it's about. The "rich" part of the title refers not only to financial wealth but wealth in life—friends, quality co–workers, a happy family. The true richness of life.

One proponent of Hill's principles was W. Clement Stone, the man I mentioned in the previous chapter whose Combined Insurance Company made millions selling insurance during the Depression. The Combined Insurance sales technique of showing local businesses name after name of other retailers in the area who had purchased insurance from the company was nothing more than Positive Mental Attitude (PMA). You've probably heard the term before, but unless you've studied it you probably didn't know what it really meant.

Napoleon Hill had a son who was born with no ears. The doctor sadly told Mr. Hill of the problem in the waiting room, and said the child would probably never be able to hear. Hill defiantly told the doctor that not only would his child hear, he would be one of the most respected people in his area. Sure enough, the prediction came true. Twice a day, Napoleon Hill would recite aloud a positive affirmation of what he envisioned for his son. He prayed for his son, and expected a miracle to occur. When the boy grew up, he did indeed have hearing, and was well-liked by everyone who knew him.

If you have never read *Think and Grow Rich*, you should, to fully grasp the power of creating a positive self-image, and a goal that you have a burning desire to achieve, like Hill had in helping his child have the gift of hearing. There is also an audio tape version available. His book *Keys to Success* is a more comprehensive method of using Hill's principles to succeed.

Napoleon Hill never set out to be a self-help guru. He came up with the idea to interview wealthy and influential people to discover the secrets of their success. He planned to write articles from the interviews and sell them to finance a law school education for himself and his brother. The first person he contacted was the billionaire industrialist Andrew Carnegie, who made a deal with Hill. He told him that if he would devote several years of his life to chronicling the successful methodologies of great entrepreneurs like himself, he would introduce him to the most influential people in America. Hill said yes, and his first interview after that was with Thomas Edison.

As he researched, Hill discovered that certain prevailing principles were mentioned over and over again by the people he interviewed, many of whom did not know each other or even share the same religious or educational background. The most common element of all was the positive mental attitude, a conviction that they not only deserved success, but had a worthwhile reason for pursuing it. People with an enthusiastic PMA kept envisioning themselves attaining their goals until the day came when they were living what they had only dreamed. Hill's first contact, Andrew Carnegie, might have been the best example. He gave away almost all his fortune to worthwhile causes. Carnegie had no self-defeating attitude about making money, and a burning desire (Hill's words) to help others with his fortune. Hill estimated that only 2 percent of the population truly achieve what they really want in life.

I've quoted motivational speaker Tony Robbins several times in my promotional literature. Robbins is a latter-day Hill. He basically followed the same path, interviewing highly influential people for their secrets and discovering that many of them followed the same basic principles of success. Then he codified it and presented it to the public, and they ate it up. He generated a lot of publicity initially by getting people to firewalk and overcome their fears, and success became a way of life for Robbins.

The Successful Attitude

Achievement begins with an attitude of success. I know. You are thinking you've heard this speech. If so, please bear with me. I believe I can share some things you may have never heard. In fact, some of the things I am going to tell you might seem far out. Just know this—I did not make these things up. Some of the principles that work for me were discovered by Napoleon Hill, then by Tony Robbins, and were taught by some of the greatest thinkers in history.

Not that I'm claiming to be one of the greatest thinkers in history, but let me ask you this:

Do you think you would like to have a million dollars?

Did that statement cause you to jump ahead of me? Have you been exposed to discussions like this and now think I am here to tell you that if you do not have a million dollars right now it is because some part of you does not want a million dollars?

Maybe that wasn't your assumption. Maybe you're thinking, "No, I want a million dollars right now. Give it to me!"

Just checking. I'm not here to shame you for not being a success. Many of the teachers, past and present, who talk about a subject like this, will tell you that if you do not have the money you want it is because of two concepts kept hidden in the dark recesses of your mind.

Bad Concept #1

Money is bad. I grew up with this idea planted in my mind, and I wouldn't be surprised if a good percentage of people who read this book don't also have this barrier to overcome. I mentioned it before: "Money is bad and the rich people got that way from stomping on poor people like us." To paraphrase that old joke about what you find between the elephants' toes (slow elephant hunters), do you know what you find on the shoe soles of rich people?

Dead poor people.

Gross, but many people have ideas like that. It's a bad concept. So is the idea that money is bad.

In reality, the idea that money is bad, is bad. Not money itself!

How do you transform your thinking about having money? Positive brainwashing! You fill your mind with stories and examples of how money has been used for good purposes. There are far, far more stories out there of how money has been used for good works. They're just not as sensational as the horror stories you get from the media, about how some pension fund has been looted by a greedy individual, or how the latest wasteful spending by Congress is about to make our taxes go up.

Let me continue a story I started earlier. The first time Ross Perot ran for President, I had heard his name but did not know much about him. When all the publicity came out about him and I learned how he made his money (providing reliable computing services to large companies and government entities), that was inspirational in itself. He saw a public need and he and his associates worked overtime, with complete devotion to their goals.

That was only half the story. I also learned about all the good things Mr. Perot had done with his money. There were stories about how he had helped better education in Texas schools. Lots of people knew the "On Wings of Eagles" story from the book that chronicled how Perot hired his own private army to rescue his people who had been captured in Iran. I learned there were many more fascinating Perot stories, though perhaps not as dramatic. As I watched these stories play over and over on TV, it began to dawn on me on a deeper level that if you have a lot of money just how much good a person can do. I know, it sounds too simplistic. Anyone should know this, but somehow, seeing the principle demonstrated in reality in Perot's life made an impact with me on some deep level. I began to think about all the good that could be done if I had plenty of money. Although I had previously thought that wealth was something I wanted to achieve, the fact that Perot's life story made such an impression on me that I had not fully grasped the impact and responsibilities of being rich.

It was after this realization that my life slowly began to change. I developed a burning desire to make a lot of money and use it for good things.

Perot's story worked for me. It may not work for you, and I don't want to take time in this book to tell you tales of Texas millionaires. You'll find your own story or personal example that will make an impact on your subconscious. Toward that end, I strongly suggest you decide to keep on the look out for stories or situations where money has been used for what the Greek philosopher Plato called **the greater good**. The more you can find of such positive stories, the better it will be for you.

If you feel you have any doubts whatsoever about whether or not it's okay to have money, you need to seek out stories like I've described. You need to spend some time specifically looking for how money was used for good. One great example in my life is Scott and Terry Paulsen. Defying conventional network marketing wisdom and people who told them they could never succeed with their revolutionary network marketing structure, they took a small investment and created Changes International. When I look at how their innovative and fair pay plan affected the lives of thousands of network marketers, helping their personal dreams come true, I think the Paulsens deserve every penny they make.

Bad Concept #2

Deep inside, are you kind of down on yourself? Do you have doubts about your own self-worth? Come on, be honest about it. I know that I did, after failing in so many programs. If you're suffering from self-abnegation (a fancy way of saying self-denial) then that could be the entire reason you haven't been a success. The bad concept that keeps many people from achieving prosperity and all the things we want in our lives is because we don't think we deserve it! For whatever reasons—and I have no intention of being your guru, psychiatrist or confessor—we think we stink. If this is your problem, make it your #1 priority to change.

How do we erase such negativity? The same way we got rid of bad concept #1. We fill our minds with information on success. Stories, books, tapes, everything you can get your hands on. At this point, I have been filling my mind with such things for years. You can find stories of successful people everywhere. I subscribe to *Forbes* and *Success* mainly so I can read about the stories of successful people. It can be very inspiring.

How powerful is your subconscious mind, the one where you have those reams of "I'm not good enough" pages stored? I have no idea what's in your mind, but I can tell you how powerful the subconscious is for me. I got over the first bad concept of thinking that money is bad when I joined Changes International and began to have all this success.

What happened then? My mind (or I should say, my subconscious) said: "Joe, you're still a bum. You don't deserve all this success, you loser. You don't deserve to have all this money, you big failure." So I created for myself a fabulously debilitating, long-lasting illness. For the first time in my life I had money to do all the things I wanted, and suddenly I was too sick to enjoy it!

It took me a long time to figure out what was wrong (a faulty self-image), so I hope by telling you this I save you some grief.

I know another successful network marketer from my years in the tape business who is always listening to motivational tapes. Dr. Wayne Dyer, Tony Robbins, Napoleon Hill, Les Brown, it doesn't matter. If it's motivational, he's there, a real believer in motivation.

I listened to the tapes every chance I had. I became a bit of a fanatic with the tapes, to the point where one day my partner got in the car with me to go somewhere and turned to me and expressed with no little emotion:

"Do you have to listen to those tapes every time you get in the car?"

After that, I became a little more moderate. When she is in the car, we listen to music, but when I am by myself I always have a motivational tape in the tape player.

Sometimes, even the title of a book or tape can make you think successfully, when you understand the concept. For example, "believe it when you see it" is a common phrase. Wayne Dyer reversed that with his *You'll See It When You Believe It*, in which he reveals how creative visualization and focusing on images of what you want to achieve can cause you to act in ways that make reality out of your thoughts.

Nightingale/Conant, based in Chicago, is the largest distributor of success and motivational tapes. I highly recommend you check out everything they and similar companies have to offer, and that you use every spare minute programing yourself for success. If it's what you need, bombarding your mind with the continuous positive mental attitudes of the people on the tapes will change your attitude on money and success.

Naturally, there are a lot more books on this subject than tapes. Visit the self–help section of your local library and bookstore and see what you can find. If you come up with something wonderful that I haven't mentioned here, please let me know about it!

Joe's Little Secret

Here is where we get into the far out part. Most people think that all memory is in the brain or mind. That is what I was taught in high school and in college. If you tell someone, "I love you with all my heart," we really know that the sentiment is really all in the brain.

Or is it?

In the May/June 1998 issue of *Intuition* magazine, an article by Hal Zina Bennett and Susan Sparrow entitled "The Thinking Heart" told how transplant recipients have inherited food cravings and much more. It described how a 52 year-old man who received the heart of a teenage boy, then began listening to ear–splitting rock music, while a 41-year-old man had visions of being killed by powerful machines, only to learn that he had received the heart of a teenage girl who was killed when her car was struck by a train. These and other stories were taken from the book *The Heart's Code* (Broadway Books, 1998) by psychologist Paul Pearsall. It includes interviews with dozens of heart and other organ transplant recipients, as well as stories from health care workers.

I'm no doctor, but I have to believe the stories in the article and book are real. In any event, I hope you get my point. John Doe has a prejudice against peanut butter so intense it seems rooted in his heart. When his heart gets replaced by one from a young girl who craves the stuff, everything is changed for John Doe. Suddenly, something for which he had great antipathy becomes worthwhile and highly desirable.

John Doe's mind has been changed by something that conventional wisdom would say is impossible. Long-standing, deeply felt emotions can be changed only by unusual situations. If you think you've been a certain way all your life—a failure at making money, perhaps—that mindset can only be changed by great effort equivalent to a heart transplant.

Call it a mind transplant if you want, but sometimes that's what it takes to effect a postive change in your life.

If you find yourself unable to succeed in network marketing, or any other type of business, as long as you're marketing a good product or service in an area where people can afford it, if you know what you're talking about and are sincere about what you're doing, if you are still not achieving your goals you may simply need to change your attitude about money. The mental equivalent of replacing John Doe's bad heart is to replace all the old, bad, worn-out anti-success, "I am not worthy" attitudes in your mind with positive ones. The only way to do that, particularly if you've spent years accumulating the bad ideas, is to bombard your mind with positive notions.

Think about it. If you've gone around for years convincing yourself of your general propensity for failure like I did, yet you've somehow managed to keep a glimmer of hope alive like I did, if you can fill your life with the positive attitudes of others, it won't be long before you'll begin believing they're right. Keep convincing yourself, and then you'll really believe them. When that happens, you won't think twice about your old self, because the new positive one will seem like the most natural thing in the world.

I'm not saying you'll have an epiphany, like I did when I realized all the good Ross Perot had done with his money, but I can assure you your life will change for the better. I'll even go so far as to tell you to love money. I mean really be in love with money, and make a commitment.

What do we do when we truly love someone? We marry them, or at least we used to do that. I've told people who I think are having a hard time that when they start making a lot of money they should have a mental marriage ceremony and marry some money. I tell them to go home, find a private place and get out a dollar, a twenty, a hundred or whatever it is that in their mind represents money.

Next, I tell them to do the following:

1. Make the money as big as they are (in their mind);
2. Take that money by the arm and walk it down the aisle;
3. Walk down that aisle right up to the preacher—whom let's say is Alan Greenspan, the wise chairman of the Federal Reserve;
4. Then, with no one objecting, they say. "I take you, money, to be my lawfully wedded spouse. To love and honor all my life.

If they kiss the money, that's their business. I don't pry into people's private lives. This little scenario always gets a few laughs, but it also gets results. Sometimes, it takes something that drastic to get a change in attitude.

Keeping Yourself and Others Inspired

Once I know that people understand the basic principles of network marketing and the pay plan I use, I refer them to sources which help keep them inspired about their own marketing abilities. Sharing my newsletters does that, but I also tell them about magazines and books that I find useful. This kind of spirit has been a staple of network marketing for years.

I believe in my "shy guy" approach and using the mail and answering phones to build a business. It's worked for me and my downline. Some people, though, like writing out scripts and making cold phone calls. Others like attending meetings and arranging meetings. You'll find how-to articles like one by Tim Sales and Leonard Atlas which describes how to overcome "fear of phoning" by working in teams to coach each other. Sales is a former member of the U.S. Navy's Underwater Explosive Ordinance Disposal Team and he and Atlas are masters at teaching people to overcome fear. So even if you don't use the same method some of the experts in the magazine like, you can still gain inspiration from their enthusiasm and wisdom.

I have often referred members of my downline to other publications that have articles like "Keeping People Involved" by Richard B. Brooke, the CEO of Oxyfresh, USA. In that article, Brooke emphasizes the point that we are not trained to keep ourselves motivated. Rather than listening to tapes or going to motivational seminars, he advises people to envision the success they desire and train themselves to think about it most of the time. Then when people get discouraged about their network marketing business (which inevitably happens with just about everyone), he reminds them about their vision and generally they become re-energized and start producing again with their original vigor. It's an age-old principle, and it works.

Napoleon Hill tells about a similar technique in his *Keys to Success*, relating the story about a man married to a realtor who has done so well she was awarded a certificate for being in the Million Dollar Club of sales commissions. Whenever she would come home after a tough day, he would pull out the certificate and ask her whose name she saw there, who it was that sold all those houses. It's all the encouragement and boost she needs to get her going again.

People who can pick themselves up by their bootstraps and put their attitudes back together after a major failure are rare. Usually, it takes a support group of some kind, or at least a single, trusted advisor or mate to get your spirits going again after you've fallen short. A lot of people who called me, and people who called the Paulsens, didn't really want information about the business. They actually wanted someone to reassure them, to pat them on the back and send them back into the fray.

That's all right and I never minded doing it, but after a while, as you absorb and deal with other's negativity, it can't help but affect you personally. That's why you need to regularly and repeatedly seek out sources of inspiration. If you already have such sources in your life and are satisfied with them, such as your religion or people you love, all the better for you. I've simply found that most people need some help, and often they need to reach some personal epiphany or breakthrough, like I reached when watching stories about the life of Ross Perot.

If I had not studied other success stories and sources of inspiration, that switch in my mind might never have been flipped when learning about Perot on television. Because a foundation had been built up over my lifetime, however, I was ready to make a change at that moment. There's an old adage that when the student is ready, the teacher arrives. Get ready!

Keep Getting Out the Good News

Since I know how easy it can be to get discouraged and give up, I take every opportunity to let people know about good news. I don't worry about sending them too much mail. When really good news comes along, I go even further. I seek out people who have become inactive and let them know, too. Just as the husband who inspired his realtor wife by showing her the Million Dollar Club certificate, or Richard Brooke of Oxyfresh reinspiring people by reminding them of their initial vision of success, I've learned that if you let people know about great recent successes they will put aside their negative ideas and give themselves (and your program) another chance.

Like building your business and improving your own attitude, it takes continual attention to maintain and improve your downline. You can't count a good harvest from any garden if you don't weed out the problems and provide nutrients on a consistent basis.

Much of what I've covered in this book is about taking care of others and seeing that they do well, which inevitably results in benefits for your own business. If you don't take care of yourself, however, you won't be there to help anyone else. That's what I'd like to cover briefly in the next chapter.

8

MAINTAINING SUCCESS

When people read my own personal story about how I had lived in apartments all my life because I couldn't afford to even rent a house, it spoke forcefully to them. They empathized when I related how I had almost been evicted, and been forced into bankruptcy only a few years before getting involved with Changes International. And when they read about how I had been able to move into a beautiful home in a mini-forest in beautiful San Marino in Southern California, some of them came to see me. After all, I didn't hesitate to say we had people making $10,000 per month out of their homes and many more making $1,000 to $5,000 selling high-quality health food supplements by mail. Some people simply wanted to thank me in person.

"Joe Brown! It's an honor to meet you!" I remember well the first time I opened the door and found an enthusiastic visitor who pumped my hand and gushed those words.

How could I blame him? I didn't turn anyone away. If someone wanted to talk about the business, I was willing to answer. Some people were content to call me, but others wanted someone to talk to, or wanted physical proof as I mentioned. They had my address, so they would stop by to say hello and talk about the pay plan, or network marketing in general. One distributor who had conducted all our transactions via mail came by just to see if I was a real person.

Because the business was so intensely interactive, I made a pact with myself to take off every working day at 5:00 to go to the gym. No matter how crazy things got, or what emergencies came up, I kept that schedule, because I knew that if I did not take care of myself, no one would be there to take care of the constant barrage of questions from people in my downline. Or at least, that's what everyone seemed to think.

I had another obligation to stay healthy—to be representative of the products we were selling. One full-color postcard showed someone winning a track meet, with the caption "How Can You Live A Healthier Life and Stay Fiscally Fit? The Answer..." And the answer was Changes International, with its revolutionary pay plan and product line and testimonials to back up everything we sold.

I worked continually to improve my mental outlook so that I could deal with the increased workload that went along with my booming success. I shared every personal realization with my downline, if I thought it was pertinent to the business. And why not? Didn't Tony Robbins tell me on a tape that the key to his success was expecting to succeed and working a lot harder than the average person? The top people in my downline who were doing very well all worked very hard, too.

Similarly, if I was selling products to help people stay more healthy, I needed to be an example of good health.

The problem was, all the motivation, enthusiasm and supplements in the world will not do you any good if you neglect the basics of good food and ample rest.

Maintaining Success

Coffee tastes good and is great at keeping a person alert, but it's a poor substitute for deep sleep and plenty of it. All the oil treatments in the world won't help a car whose engine needs an overhaul.

In 1996 my health began to fail. At first I ignored the warning signs, but eventually I realized I had to seek medical help. By early 1997 I began telling the people who received my newsletters something that those who stayed in close contact with me already knew or suspected—my health was not the best. The truth was, although my level of income stayed steady due to (a) the business I had built, (b) the soundness of the Changes International pay plan and products, and (c) excellent producers in my downline, I was unable to devote more than a few hours a week to my business due to a panoply of physical problems. I could do little more than get out a monthly newsletter and do far less phone and mailing work than I had done previously. In my September 1997 letter I stated it flatly:

"As many of you know, I have not been feeling well for the past several months and I have been able to give very little time to the downline I built or continue building."

I don't want to bore you with all that was wrong with me. Suffice it to say that, basically, in my zeal to build a business and make sure that every single distributor or potential distributor I came in contact with was satisfied every time they contacted me with a problem, I neglected my own well-being. Sure, I went to the gym every day and worked out, but that could not compensate for long-term sleep deprivation and less than adequate attention to my own dietary needs. It's one thing to have great supplements and nutritional products, but they are just that—supplemental. They are not *fundamental*, and I had neglected the basic foundations of good health.

By late spring of 1998, I was able to report to my downline that I was making good progress with my health situation, so much so that I could focus on new ideas for mail and phone systems and entertain the possibility of doing conference calls and traveling to meetings.

Thank goodness for the "shy guy" system I developed! Had I been involved in normal methods of network marketing work—opportunity meetings, conventions, sales training workshops, heavy cold-calling with scripted presentations—my goose would have been cooked when my health nose-dived. And who knows? I've never been the athletic type, anyway. Due to my insistence on taking the best care possible of people working with me, I might have driven myself into the ground far more quickly if I had been athletic and in tiptop shape when my business started taking off. But all I was doing was working out of my home, sending out mailings and taking phone calls. Why was that so tough?

There's an old joke about a farmer, a surgeon, and a network marketer talking about whose job has been around the longest.

The farmer grins, hoists up the straps of his overalls with his thumbs, and proudly proclaims that in the beginning Adam and Eve were in a garden. "That means Adam must have been a farmer," he says, "so naturally I have the oldest profession."

"Ah, that's where you're wrong," says the physician. "To make Eve, God took a rib from Adam's side. Since that's surgery, obviously the oldest profession is a surgeon, like me."

Of course, the network marketer says he can't agree with that, which baffles the farmer and surgeon, so he explains. "In Genesis, it says that before God created the world, the earth was without form and void."

"So? What does that have to do with a profession?" asks the farmer.

"What's another way of saying 'without form and void'?" asks the network marketer.

"Confusion?" says the surgeon.

"Precisely," the network marketer replies. "And who do you think created the confusion? A network marketer!"

Building a network marketing business has its own built-in confusions, and every single person who comes into the business, no matter how experienced they are at network marketing, has some initial misunderstandings. It's just human nature. When you deal with confusion on a constant basis, it can wear away at you, and if you don't watch yourself, you'll keep plunging on without rest, trying to quell the uproar in your life. It can make you sick, literally.

No doubt, if you're interested enough in network marketing to read a book like this, you're someone who is willing to work hard to give yourself a business in which you make your own dress code, set your own hours, and pursue the best chance possible for an average person today to make a substantial part-time or even full-time income. I simply advise you to not do so at the expense of your own health. People in your downline will, if you let them, not read materials, not listen to tapes, not attend meetings, and not do research on their own. As long as they know they can pick up the phone and call you, or even come over to see you, at all hours of the day and night, with any single (even trivial) question they might dream up, they will do so. It can get very, very emotionally draining when it seems like you're continually rewinding and replaying the same tape, hour after hour, day after day.

In essence, that's what happened with me. Maybe I got so caught up with all the uproar and skyrocketing business, I was able to focus on the business but lost sight of everything else in my life, including my own well-being. Don't let something like that happen to you. Set up a schedule and do your utmost to keep it, and I don't mean simply working out every day at a set time like I did, if that means you'll then come back to the office and lose all the benefits you've gained by working yourself into oblivion.

If you've chosen the right kinds of leaders for your downline, they'll pick up the slack. You might have to show them several times what you have in mind, but eventually they'll get it. If they don't, and prefer to simply keep pestering you with the same old problems after you've given them workable solutions, or they send people to you with a "Go ask Joe" attitude when the answers are right there in material already available, who needs that kind of distributor, anyway? Believe me, if you're willing to let go of something that is less than what you really want, you might find that the vacuum which results will be replaced by something much better.

In his book *Keys to Success*, Napoleon Hill says that anything that affects the soundness of your mind will affect your body, and vice versa. If you believe that, it follows that if your body is adversely stressed by sleep deprivation or bad dietary habits, your mind will be next. Then you have a downward spiral that any airplane pilot will tell you is very difficult to pull out of. Hill also stresses that the subconscious mind will work for you while the conscious mind is at rest. He cites the example of Archimedes struggling for a solution to determining the relative mass of two objects. The philosopher gave up and took a hot bath, only to realize that the solution lay in how his body displaced the water, giving rise to his famous cry of "Eureka!" (I have found it).

There are better ways to solve your problems, or those of people who depend upon you, than by working yourself into ill health. Many people have found that, just before they go to sleep, if they tell their subconscious to give them a solution to a problem, they'll have the answer when they wake up. While the conscious mind is resting, the never-weary subconscious keeps on working away.

As Napoleon Hill says in *Keys to Success*:

"Your mind and your body are the navigator and the ship which carry you to the success you deserve. Do everything you can to preserve, protect, and defend them."

You may achieve network marketing success as great or greater than my own. Just make sure you keep yourself healthy enough to enjoy it!

9

SEVEN SIMPLE STEPS TO SUSTAINED SUCCESS

It took me a long time to find the right network marketing program for me. Despite its innovation, fairness and stability, Changes International by no means cornered the market on network marketing of health products. Ford might make the best automobiles this year, but next year they might be subject to a government recall. People and companies change, so you have to stay alert about the entire marketplace and what is available that most perfectly suits your unique needs and abilities. Nevertheless, I feel there are seven elements that should be considered in evaluating any network marketing program that comes your way. These are guidelines that seem obvious, even simple, but they took me years to work out, both before and after I joined Changes International.

SIMPLE STEP #1: LEARN ABOUT THE PAY PLAN

A company could offer the greatest new product in the universe, have the personal endorsement of the President of the United States, and show you expensively–produced videos with real Hollywood movie stars enjoying tropical vacations they've won as a result of being involved in a particular network marketing program, and it won't mean a single thing to you. If you cannot easily understand the pay plan and **GET INTO PROFIT QUICKLY,** with minimal involvement and investment, with real potential for much larger rewards down the line, that network marketing program is meaningless. The go–getter who can make any program boom is a very small percentage of the network marketing population. A larger percentage need minimal supervision and inspiration to succeed. At least 2/3 of all network marketers, however, need a good deal of help to make the business work. So the more complex the pay plan, the harder it will be to understand. **IF PEOPLE CANNOT START MAKING MONEY FAIRLY QUICKLY** and easily once they sign up, your dropout rate will give you more headaches than they make aspirin to handle. Perhaps the biggest reason people drop out is the pay plan. A great number of people live from paycheck to paycheck, so when they invest even a couple of hundred dollars in buying into a program, they need to recoup their investment quickly. They need to make money right away, or it's not worth investing their time.

On the other hand, if they can invest 5 to 15 hours of their time each week, have no problem explaining the pay plan to potential distributors, and make even a small profit rather quickly, their chances of staying in a program are greatly improved.

Don't simply compare the first few levels of a program with other programs you understand. That's what I did when I got involved with Changes International. I did not expect to make the big money on the back end (the Leadership Bonus) because I had never done that with other programs.

Other programs weren't like Changes, but I didn't understand that going in. After I was involved, though, I was able to explain how the Leadership Bonus was much better than the top end compensation of other programs.

We are fast approaching the time when as many as 50 percent of all U.S. households will be engaged in some form of home office activity. The computer revolution, corporate downsizing, economic downturns, and people's strong desire to be their own boss and set their own hours have all contributed to this phenomenon. Even people who have thriving regular businesses, like the surgeon mentioned in the *Success* magazine article, are getting into network marketing and running that business out of a home office (in that case, the surgeon's wife partnered with him in their network marketing business). Network marketing today is a $70+ billion per year business, and one of the leading reasons for the home office movement. It offers a way for companies to move products directly to the consumer without a dozen other middle steps, saving on shipping, staffing, and mainstream media advertising costs.

Distributors make money in two ways: (a) by buying products from the company at wholesale prices and selling them at retail; and (b) sponsoring distributors into their downline and receiving commissions and bonuses on the monthly purchases made by everyone underneath them in the resulting multi-level market structure. It only follows that everyone in that structure should understand exactly how and when they get paid.

There are basically three types of pay plans in use in network marketing. The first is the "Break Away." It has qualifications that a distributor must attain before making money. Then, once they are on top, they have to meet other criterion in order to get bonuses. These qualifications are usually quite high, and thus the "heavy-hitters" and Type A personalities are generally the only people who make it to the top of a Break Away.

The Forced Matrix is a plan which promises a big spillover of profits after you get a large number of people in your downline. You have to have great persistence and the ability to convince others to stick it out for the long haul, and hope that the company using this plan survives in the interim.

The third type of plan is called a Binary. The basic idea is to keep two groups balanced in group volume. If you have a masochistic nature and want to see just what it takes to burn yourself out, try this one. You'll have to spend hour after hour on the phone talking about the volume of sales they are doing, and then figure out how to manipulate things so that the two sides of the Binary sales scale stay balanced so that you can get your commission.

Lucky for me, the Changes International plan is none of the above.

A Comparison

Let's compare again the difference between the percentage of payout from the typical network marketing pay plan and that of Changes International. Whatever type of plan they are using, many companies pay only 5 percent to 10 percent commission and spread that compensation out over many levels. The more levels there are, the more people you have to have in your downline before you start making a profit, and due to recruiting lags, the time before you will get paid can stretch out over several months.

Most people new to network marketing, at least those who get into the typical program, find "normal" pay structures confusing, so they "just sell the product and let the pay plan take care of itself." Naturally, it rarely does, because that's a bit like saying "Just take the trip and let the road take care of directions."

Let's look at your Typical Pay Plan.

**Your Downline
Your Earnings**

Level 1 distributors
   5-10 percent
   (People you personally sponsor)
   commission on purchases

Level 2 distributors
   5-10 percent
   (People your level 1 distributors personally sponsor) commission on purchases

Level 3 distributors
   5-10 percent
   (People your level 2 distributors personally sponsor) commission on purchases

Level 5 distributors
   5-10 percent
   (People your level 4 distributors personally sponsor) commission on purchases

Level 6 distributors
   5-10 percent
   (People your level 5 distributors personally sponsor) commission on purchases

Seems simple enough, doesn't it? If you think so, sit down with a pad of paper and a pencil and start doing some hypotheticals on 20 people in a downline under the structure given above. Based on a $100 per month basic volume (BV), see if you can keep track of all the percentages and figure out how much money you would be due. Or, if you'd like to see a far better pay plan, take a look at the following example of a Changes International program, based on a downline of 4 first level and 16 second level distributors, each also selling around $100BV each month. Here's the Changes International Pay Plan:

**Your Downline
Your Earnings**

Level 1 distributors
15 percent
*(People you personally sponsor)
commission on monthly purchases*

Level 2 distributors
45 percent
(People your level 1 distributors personally sponsor) commission on monthly purchases

Level 3 distributors
up to 15 percent Leadership Bonus
(People your level 2 distributors personally sponsor) commission on monthly purchases

As you can no doubt see from the difference in the first two levels only, the difference in 5–10 percent and 15 percent on the first level is substantial. The difference in 5–10 percent and 45 percent on the second level is stunning, which is why so many people pooh–poohed the Changes International plan when it first debuted. They said it could never ever work, or someone would have come up with it long ago.

They were wrong, and I didn't have to run many numbers to see how quickly I could break even and get into profit on only the first two levels of the Changes plan.

THE PROGRAM WAS SPECIFICALLY DESIGNED SO THE AVERAGE DISTRIBUTOR COULD START MAKING MONEY ALMOST IMMEDIATELY, WITH VERY FEW PEOPLE IN THEIR DOWNLINE.

Now that there are other companies trying to emulate the Changes structure, if you keep up with the network marketing world this pay plan might not seem unusual to you, but at the time it came out, it was manna from Heaven, an network marketer's dream.

Since there are so many network marketing programs out there and they change every day, I won't attempt to give you a real example of what you can make in another type of program, but I can give you some realistic examples of what you could potentially make under the Changes International pay plan.

Example A

Let's say you personally sponsor four distributors on your first level and earn 15 percent on their "Six Pack," which is any combination of six bottles of product. Each Changes bottle, of any product, sells for approximately the same price, which is another reason the figures are simple to calculate. Let's say a distributor buys bottles costing $18.67. So, buying six bottles (total cost $112.02) means you stay in "Active" status as a distributor because you have purchased at least $100 Business Volume (BV) in that given month. A purchase of six bottles also qualifies you as an "Executive" and enables you to be paid 15 percent on the BV of all "Active" First Level Distributors. You are also to be paid 45 percent on the BV of all "Active" Second Level distributors and qualify to participate in the Third Level to Leadership Bonus Program.

If you only purchase three bottles of product during the commission month, that qualifies you as a "Jr. Executive" and you are paid 10 percent on the BV of all Active First Level distributors in your downline, as well as 25 percent on the BV of all Active Second Level distributors.

A Junior Executive does not qualify for the Leadership Bonus.

For simplicity, let's calculate the following percentages on a $100BV.

If you have four Active distributors on your First Level and you have qualified as an Executive, you receive 15 percent on their purchases that month.

First Level Commission = 4 x $15 = $60 profit. If each of these four First Level distributors sponsors four new First Level distributors each (16 total), that becomes your Second Level and as an Executive you get 45 percent on their Six Pack purchases.

Second Level Commission = 16 x $45 = $720 profit

Example B
Now let's say you personally sponsor an even dozen Active distributors on your First Level and you earn 15 percent on their purchases that month.

First Level Commission = 12 x $15 = $180 profit. We'll also say that these twelve First Level distributors sponsors eight new First Level distributors each (96 total), and that becomes your Second Level. Since you get 45 percent on their Six Pack purchases, your Second Level Commission = 96 x $45 = $4,320 profit. If you had 12 First Level distributors in your downline, you would be qualified to receive a 15 percent Third Level to Leadership Bonus, as long as all those people are purchasing at least $100BV of products each month. Many people would be very happy making $4,500 per month, period, but this should give you some idea of how the numbers can add up quickly.

The Leadership Bonus Marketing Plan
Any Changes distributor qualifies for the Leadership Bonus by having 3, 6, 9 or 12 personally sponsored First Level distributors who are purchasing at least $100BV of products each month. Third Level to Leadership Bonuses are shared among Executives.

4-Star Executives also receive 2 percent down through three generations of 4-Star Executives. Of course, the examples listed above are based on Executive status and are not promises or guarantees of income. They only represent simple examples of potential earnings.

The key here is that getting bonuses under this system is much easier to obtain than in most network marketing pay plans.

In case you're wondering, the suggested retail prices of most Changes International product bottles is $29.95, so there is ample room for profit that way as well. And remember, these are all renewable products. For example, the suggested use for the *Thermolift* Herbal Energizer Super Fat Burner capsules was two per day, one in the morning and another in the afternoon, which meant a new bottle was needed each month. At one time, Changes also sold a "Business in a Box" for $149 (distributor price) which included one bottle each of their six products at the time, a pack of each of the brochures, a pack of ten *Thermolift* sample, a New Distributor Training Kit, and a camera–ready Distributor Application and Order Form. The price included all shipping and handling charges.

All told, the Changes plan offers a potential payout of 81 percent and an average actual payout of 62 percent. In contrast, the average actual payout of the entire network marketing industry is only 25–30 percent, which is about half of what most companies claim their potential is. The difference goes into the pockets of the people who own the other network marketing companies. If it appears that a company not using a pay plan like Changes is working on a 40 percent profit margin, the likely reality is that they are actually enjoying a 70 percent profit margin.

I hope that makes you see why the network marketing industry stacked the tables against the new distributor before the revolutionary Changes International pay plan.

In summary, the Changes pay plan was fair and easy to understand, the price to get involved was relatively low, and the profits for those who produced came quickly, without waiting months for a huge downline to grow.

I suggest you look for a similar situation with any network marketing company you consider joining or starting. You need good products at a good price, but the pay plan is crucial. I was involved with lots of network marketing programs before Changes International, some of them selling very similar products. Funny, but I never found a single one where the pay plan took care of itself.

SIMPLE STEP #2: DON'T BUY THE HYPE

There's a reason why preventative health maintenance has become such a huge industry in the United States. Diet products are a staple of network marketing companies for the same reason. Baby Boomers. As the generation that grew up watching "The Mickey Mouse Club" on TV grows older, middle–age spread and the encroaching troubles of age become a reality. In addition, the Woodstock Generation also heavily explored things their parents barely knew about, like yoga and nutritional supplements.

With the Social Security system looking increasingly precarious, many Baby Boomers wonder if they will ever see any retirement money from the government, or have Medicare to fall back on if necessary. Therefore, preventative maintenance makes sense, because it's easier to live a happy life if you're healthy, particularly in your "golden years." Network marketing also offers people a chance to serve these concerns and make a great part–time income.

Unfortunately, any generation that grows up watching television runs the risk of being brainwashed by Madison Avenue, and I don't mean the "positive brainwashing" I discussed in the chapter on motivation. What I'm talking about is the celebrity spokesperson, or ads that appeal to your vanity. Maybe you've been personally involved with some here–today, gone–tomorrow dietary company. Any stable company like Changes International has people at the top who care about the long–term survival of the program and their distributors. Something may come along and be the latest rage, but I always approach such programs with a skeptical eye.

I tell people in my downline to investigate any possibility they find, and if it's good, to tell me about it. I also don't trust the latest thing until I thoroughly investigate it and personally try it.

Don't buy the hype. Hucksterism is what gave network marketing a bad name in the first place, and it took many years and a lot of good work to get the industry where it is today, in the land of respectability. Help us keep it there for those who will follow.

SIMPLE STEP #3: A HOT PRODUCT WILL NOT MAKE YOU RICH BY ITSELF

Changes International never sold any one particularly flashy "flagship" product. At the time of this printing, Changes' most popular item, the thermogenic weight loss product *Thermolift*, had sold 3,000,000 bottles because it works. Composed of chromium picolinate and the herbs ma huang, guarana and white willow, it supports an increase in the body's basal metabolic rate (the number of calories a body burns in a day). The effects of chromium picolinate on weight loss are well–known. Ma huang is a staple herb of the Chinese world, while guarana is a caffeine–rich herb from South America. White willow's active ingredients are salicylates, like we find in aspirin. The use of chromium picolinate is relatively new, but the herbs in *Thermolift* have been used in various cultures around the world for thousands of years. A new name, a new combination perhaps. Nothing so startling that you could build a company on it, but the product does work great because we sold over 3,000,000 bottles at $18.67 (the price Changes charges distributors).

Accordingly, you cannot expect as a sole distributor, even if you bring a sizable downline with you to a new network marketing company, to get rich off a single product. You might be thinking that 3,000,000 bottles of *Thermolift* at $29.95 (the retail price of Changes' products) is $89,850,000, but remember that those millions were spread out among 100,000 or so Changes distributors.

About a decade ago, network marketers sold water purifiers for kitchens and other "one-time only" products. There was a great deal of public concern over drinking water purity at the time, and the companies selling the devices made a substantial amount of money. When the market was saturated, they marketed air purifiers and other similar devices, but the hype necessary to sell the first device left a lasting impression in the minds of consumers and distributors, particularly when said devices did not meet promised levels of reliability.

I can't fault anyone for getting on board with a winning product. If you're lucky enough to be one of the first people involved in the company and know how to build a downline, you can do very, very well. But what happens when the company hits a market saturation point? Even if you are selling renewable products—one particular miracle diet product, for example—if something goes wrong with the product, or demand is such that your orders cannot be filled in a timely fashion, your whole business might quickly fall apart.

With few exceptions, no one hot product will make you rich all by itself. You need a company with several reliable, renewable products that work well and will keep working long into the future. If you have that, your reputation and your downline are not threatened if that single product does not meet up to expectations

Think long-term diversity, and you can't go wrong.

SIMPLE STEP #4: BE WILLING TO FAIL

I recounted my own story, and briefly mentioned the background of great leaders like Abraham Lincoln. In any business, it is more usual than not for business people to mail many times before striking a success. Even when start-ups become massive successes the first time out, there are still nightmares awaiting. The story of Mrs. Fields' Cookies is a prime example. Debbie Fields took a single store to a worldwide company more quickly than was prudent and got in debt over her ears. When she franchised her stores rather than trying to personally run a chain, she got back into profit. Scott and Terry Paulsen brought decades of experience into the formation of Changes International, some in network marketing and some in the normal world of business. Obviously, everything they touched had not turned to gold, or they wouldn't have started Changes in the first place. Based on their own experience and armed with a revolutionary but untried idea, they were willing to take a chance. If they tried and failed, so be it. At least they would have given it the old college try. They were willing to risk substantial resources and time on something they believed in.

The trick about failing is learning from your failures. For the longest time, I thought my network marketing losses were due to some personal quirk or sad fate that I had been assigned. Other times I wondered if it was really possible to make money at network marketing if you had a personality like mine. As I approached the age of 50, I thought that I might die an old man, mostly a failure at everything. Then one day I learned that the reason I had been failing at network marketing—and the reason that I kept coming back despite a jillion reasons not to—**was that the odds of most pay plans were simply stacked against me**. Once I found a fair, easily-understood pay plan and a program that would allow me to do the marketing my way, defeat quickly transformed into victory.

Compared to all my failures, my success with Changes International is the difference between the guy in the lead convertible waving to screaming crowds at a ticker tape down Fifth Avenue in New York and the aching street worker going along behind the people and the cars, slowly sweeping up the mountains of confetti.

With no offense meant to street sweepers, unlike that imaginary guy I never gave up. I was willing to fail, time after time, but I always had at least a glimmer of a hope that one day it could be me in that shiny convertible. Sometimes I think that if you keep coming back again and again, learning a little here, a little there, you reach a point where one day the forces that oppose you, be they ignorance or economic background or lack of education, all finally give up, and you have a breakthrough that you deserve, if for no other reason than you just wouldn't give up. The universe respects someone who will not quit.

And as I said earlier, every book that I've ever read on success says that the most important ingredient in the lives of successful people is that they expect to have happen what they want to have happen. They're so convinced of it that they keep coming back, picking themselves up off the floor and continuing, every time they fail. They are willing to fail.

You can't recruit every person you contact into your downline. You can't expect to keep all your top producers happy, or keep them from moving on to other network marketing companies. The quickest way to replace a swelled ego with humility is to be doing well then suddenly take a dive. When you fall hard enough, it makes you back away from yourself and assess your real strengths and weaknesses. And every time you go back at your goal, you're a little stronger and the path gets a little easier.

If you're not willing to fail at all, though, it's doubtful you'll ever make it. So be willing to fail.

SIMPLE STEP #5: DEVELOP YOUR OWN WORKABLE SYSTEM

Do you truly know your own strengths and personality? If you do, building a system that reflects what you're all about should not be hard, and you'll probably attract others like yourself. My "shy guy" system might not work as well for others as it did for me. I could see that early on, and so I've always urged people to try any personal system that makes sense to them. If anyone tells you that their way of doing network marketing is the only way that truly works, walk the other way. Network marketing changes all the time. If the Paulsens had listened to the "conventional wisdom" of their friends and business associates, they would never have built Changes International. If I had listened to other successful network marketing people I knew when I got involved in Changes, I would never have developed the three-step, mail-based system that worked so well for me. No one has ever joined my downline because they thought my way of doing things was the best way in the universe. Every single person has some unique quirk in the way they go about building a business.

In one booklet, Changes recommends to their distributors that the simplest and least expensive way to promote their business is to contact their "warm market," meaning their friends or acquaintances who are currently involved in network marketing. As I said, my friends never listened to me, pre–Changes or post–Changes. Well, maybe they listen to me a little bit now, but my family still hasn't gotten involved in network marketing. If I had concentrated on the first group recommended by Changes, I might never have built my business.

We do agree on one thing, however. Every individual's own time and effort is the key factor in determining their level of success in network marketing. Like water, I believe they have to find their own level.

My own system went through several changes. At one time I tried postcards, then I learned that several pages of mailings worked better. That evolved into my phenomenally successful booklet, *The Secrets of Network Marketing Revealed*. My two–minute introductory tape was literally heard around the world, but no one coached me in recording it. Similarly, another very popular tape was a recorded phone conversation of myself and Scott Paulsen, also done casually.

You simply have to develop a system that works for you. If you love speaking in front of groups, more power to you. I was just never inclined that way. I also never liked "working the phones," but you might love it.

I can't emphasize enough, however, that whatever system you develop, if you intend to pass it on to everyone in your downline, it must be capable of being easily and fully understood by any average person.

Seven Simple Steps to Sustained Success

Dave Colbert, a highly successful network marketer who made the Shaklee 1 percent Club and ten years later started NuImage International, calls such a method a "unified duplicatable system." In his "Details of a Network Marketing Millionaire" video series, he suggests that your system be designed to keep people involved, and that no hype or personal example will work because personality is not duplicatable. Only principles can be understood, Colbert claims, and I agree.

The Changes International pay plan took enormous amounts of money that normally went only to the heavy–hitters and spread it out among everyone else. If you have a good pay plan and a good company, don't get in your own way by coming up with a system that works very well for you but cannot be easily explained to everyone else.

Sometimes, the old KISS principle (Keep It Simple, Stupid) works best. One distributor discovered that a lot of network marketers were dissatisfied with the wholesale prices they were paying for products. They thought they were paying way too much, and they were right. He began running simple little ads that compared the prices of Changes products to those of other network marketing companies. Not emphasis on distributor retention rate, or revolutionary pay plan. Just "this is what our products cost; this is what their products cost." Experienced network marketers responded in droves.

You don't have to use elaborate prose or thousand–dollar ads to be very successful in network marketing. All you need is something that anyone else can read, understand, and put into action. If that means a mail-based system or a script for making cold calls over the phone, if it works for you and you can teach it to others easily, you'll probably do well.

SIMPLE STEP #6: DO YOUR RESEARCH BEFORE YOU JOIN

Multi-level marketing today is a billion dollar industry in the United States. It has been around for over forty years, and offers life-changing success for people from all walks of life. By and large, relatively little investment is needed to get started, and an MBA is not a prerequisite to putting together your own, thriving company. Nevertheless, the vast majority of the American public have little idea what the terms "network marketing" or "MLM" mean. That's why new distributors get burned by fly-by-night companies every single day, and then refuse to look at another program, thinking they've had one brush with the industry and suddenly know how every other company in the business works.

Yet do you know of any other industry where people can earn five figure monthly incomes within months of joining a company? Is there any other business which allows you to multiply your efforts by rewarding you from the earnings of every single person active in your organization? In the literature I send my people I tell them that only in network marketing can you:

1. Start part-time from your home without the risk of losing your present income;

2. Start a business with a very small, affordable investment;

3. Enjoy virtually unlimited income potential;

4. Suffer no limitations on your business due to territory, age, sex, or season;

5. Enter the business with no special skills or training;

6. Operate with very low overhead and no employees.

Now this is all well and good, but no matter how effective you are at building a business, if you're in business with a company that does not care about your long-term well-being, you're in big trouble. Every company supplies a Distributor Application & Agreement, which all look relatively the same, but what about the Terms & Conditions page that accompanies the Agreement? If you took time to read it (I don't know many people who do), would you discover that you are severely limited with regard to legal recourse, should anything go wrong due to faulty products or false claims by the company?

It's easy to forget such considerations, when you have big checks waved in your face. That makes it easy to overlook the details that matter, One reason why I quit sending out copies of my checks was because I realized that for many people the focus shifted to big checks and only big checks. The reputation of the company, the workability of the pay plan, and the quality of the products fell by the wayside in the pursuit of the big check.

This is precisely why you must do thorough research, and not simply trust the dazzle of a big check. It's easy to get mesmerized by a heavy-hitter at a meeting who is wearing a thick gold ring and a Rolex President watch. Maybe you saw him drive into the parking lot in his new BMW, or saw her designer gown shimmer when she purposely walked under the big lights on her way to the podium. Hype exists on many levels.

I still send out postcards, but I don't emphasize the size of the checks I receive. Instead, I state how *many* checks our company mailed out in the last month. Imagine reading "12,000+ Checks Sent Out Last Month...And you could have received one of them! Work for a company where you actually get paid!"

Wouldn't that get your attention? The emphasis is on the fact that a lot of people are making money, not just some fat cat pulling down six figures.

You can do your research, poring over back issues of the major magazines dedicated to network marketing. You can try to find friends and relatives who have been involved in network marketing, and might know some hot gossip about a company you're considering. You could read testimonials and try to get in touch with the person advocating the company. You could even call your local Better Business Bureau and see if they have anything on file.

There's an easier way. I start by telling people that prior to its merger with Twin Labs, Changes International was privately–owned and debt–free. Then I tell them that from its start, the company wanted to enable the average person to be financially successful.

Not just successful in network marketing, but financially successful overall. More specifically:

> "The goal of Changes International is to allow anyone with a little ambition to earn a substantial monthly income with a small downline of only 30–50 distributors."

Then I tell them that if any network marketing company is *really* offering a legitimate opportunity, one thing *must* be true. That company must have a high distributor retention rate. I tell them most network marketing companies have only a 10–15 percent annual retention rate, meaning they lose 85–90 percent of their new distributors each year. Not that I like being redundant, but some people don't really get it until I flip the percentages. Then I tell them that Changes has a noticeably high annual distributor retention rate, and that is why they have had such an amazing, continuing success. Anyone can understand that such a low dropout rate can only mean one thing—a high percentage of the distributors are making money. Talk about duplicatable! When I go over the compensation plan, I'm doing it to a dedicated audience.

I went to a seminar once where several highly gifted and personable people were describing their previous experience with other network marketing companies. They had recruited hundreds of people but had received miserably small monthly checks, compared to the effort they had expended. As soon as they got into a "distributor friendly" company, each of them ended up making monthly checks in the six-figure range!

This taught me that if highly skilled people could not make the grade with a tricky marketing plan, average people certainly could not. So any time you learn about a new network marketing opportunity, use the simple criterion of finding out (a) whether or not the company has been around for a substantial length of time; and if so (b) their annual distributor retention rate.

Sometimes you might discover a brand-new company with what looks like a fair pay plan and good products, put together by experienced network marketing executives. If they have little track record as a company, there's always one good way to determine if their worthwhile, and it doesn't take a lot of research on your part.

"What is your annual distributor retention rate?" That's all you need to ask to find out if people are being treated fairly and making money and sticking around for the long haul.

SIMPLE STEP #7: HELP YOUR DOWNLINE, HELP YOURSELF

I've told you a number of stories about how my emphasis in building my business was always on helping my downline first, at times even to my own detriment. Even when I battled health problems, I still managed to get out a monthly newsletter that shared every tip I could come up with and offered words of encouragement along with news of other distributors' successful techniques. I always mentioned books, magazines, videos, and cassettes if I thought there was something there from which the people in my downline could benefit.

The helpful spirit pervades my downline. One sheet that I distribute now offers a list of phone numbers around the country. There is my two-minute message, both at my own business line and another distributor's office on the east coast. Another phone line offers Saturday training classes in which people share selling techniques, while another lists all ongoing conference and training calls.

My top distributor, Barbara Wright, put together a Product Chat on another line.

Another distributor has a phone line featuring interviews with company leaders offering tips on how they built their business. On Tuesday, Wednesday and Friday nights between 7:30 and 10:30 p.m. EST you can call the same number to hear "Opportunity Calls" from new prospects.

When Twin Labs and Changes merged, we offered an 800 number that got folks a pre-recorded message from Ross Blechman, the president & CEO of Twin Labs, to all distributors. This great message is very popular, and in the tradition of the President's Hot Line number.

Anyone who has anything to contribute that is helpful is always welcomed with open arms. One distributor put together an outline for cold calling prospects. It is not just a script to follow, but an explanation of the logic behind the script. I don't use it, because making cold calls isn't how I did business, but those distributors of mine who felt differently make use of it.

And all the most helpful tools eventually made their way, even if only briefly mentioned, into the Changes International New Distributor Manual.

In April 1998 an article about Changes appeared in AdNet's *Network Opportunities: The Magazine for Professional Networkers*. The article first described the three basic principles of the company:

1. quality products that fulfill a growing market demand;
2. a compensation plan that rewards new distributors quickly; and
3. a supportive team environment.

"We believe in offering great products, giving people great earning potential and helping them feel good about their work," Scott told the magazine.

The article went on to explain how, after the merger with Twin Labs, Changes had introduced a number of new products and how Twin Labs had invested hundreds of thousands of dollars to give Changes a greatly improved computer system. After explaining how the Changes pay plan worked, readers came to a sub-headline that read: *People Make Changes Successful.*

"It's our people that really make us an exceptional company," Terry Paulsen said. "The assistance doesn't just come in the form of a workbook. At Changes, our distributors are part of a team that's always available to help people reach their goals. New distributors have meaningful access to seasoned networkers. Through mentoring relationships, Changes really helps you as you work to make positive changes in your life. We'll help you set—and reach—your goals, and we'll stick with you through the ups and downs along the way."

Boy, was he ever right with that last statement. When I read that, I thought about my own tough times, and how people had stood by me when I was in little shape to do more than try and get well. The checks had kept coming in, and no one had ever complained. I couldn't help but think that all my efforts in network marketing had paid off, even the failures. I had learned something from everything, and when I'd finally found a program that was fair, through which my own personality and methods could blossom, I had reached the prosperity of my dreams. The more I had helped my downline, the more I had succeeded.

I couldn't have done it any other way.

10
SYSTEMS OF THE FUTURE

Like most businesses, network marketing has to keep evolving to stay viable. It has changed drastically over my years in network marketing, and most of the changes have been quite positive. Originally, most network marketing companies were arranged so that the supervisor (or whatever other title the top of a network was called) was sponsored directly by the company and received all the product for their entire downline. The supervisor then passed the product on down, level by level. Paychecks worked the same way. The top dog got paid for all the sales in their downline and they had to in turn write checks for everyone.

As you might imagine, this was very time-consuming. It was also a big temptation and opportunity for fraud. Many times, those on bottom levels never received even the small checks they earned.

Fortunately for those entering network marketing today, everything is computerized, particularly the checks. All checks come directly from the company to your mailbox, and most companies have sophisticated computer software to actually keep track of everything.

Other traditions have continued. For years, network marketing was simply word of mouth, a person–to–person selling method that worked well for outgoing personalities but was murder on someone not so inclined. Word of mouth is still big in network marketing, but the many new ideas that have been initiated in recent years are more appealing to most folks. These include advertising, co–op advertising, cassette tapes, video tapes, conference calls, etc. I have used and modified some of these ideas to build my business.

Phone/Fax Systems

That brings us to the network marketing company of the future. Like many other businesses, network marketing is moving in an electronic direction. Common elements of many programs now are 90% automated voice mail, recorded 24–hour messages that anyone can listen to at their convenience, and very complete fax on demand. Fax on demand is particularly interesting, because it lets someone call a phone number and pick only the documents they want to see. It is narrow casting as opposed to the broadcasting approach of sending every prospect the very same material in the mail.

Here is how it works. A distributor runs ads or mails postcards offering the opportunity to "earn money working from home." When someone responds to the ad by calling, they are referred to a toll–free number. This toll–free number offers a recording which gives the whole "sales pitch" over the phone. The caller then hears a menu of options and can listen to any or all of the pre–recorded phone messages and by entering the numbers they pick, have several pages of information faxed to the number they designate.

This system eliminates one of the main reason people fail in network marketing, and that is that people simply do not want to sell. In essence, the recorded message/fax on demand system does all the selling for you.

The problem with these systems is that they have to be very good. They really must be very convincing—at least as compelling as my popular two-minute message that was heard around the world. Also, you have the problem of different strokes for different folks. Some people calling in only want to listen for a minute or two. Others are willing to listen for 20 minutes as long as they like what they are hearing. This means you think about what you put on your system. You have to design your voice and fax system to satisfy both types of individuals, and this can be tricky. People have all kinds of comfort zones. Some people want to be called back and talk to a human, just as I wanted to talk to Scott Paulsen when I first heard about Changes International. Other people do not want anyone to call and try to "sell" them and turn off the minute they hear from you.

Like I said, out of necessity every industry keeps evolving. Many people in network marketing are in the process of refining these voice/fax systems, and I don't know of anyone who has a perfect, foolproof setup that will please everyone.

Nevertheless, people are still being fooled. You can have a "GREAT SYSTEM" and recruit lots of people, but if the pay plan is bad most individuals will still not make a significant income. That's one reason I wanted to write this book and get it read by as many people as possible. There are thousands and thousands of people each month wanting to get into a mail order, work from your home business. Most of these new people get taken in by these new systems which claim to be no-brainers. They don't realize that no recruiting system negates the importance of pay plans.

Of course, every company claims to have the best pay plan.

So how is the new person to know?

That is the problem. They can not. As I made clear early on, there is no network marketing college. The only way anyone can truly learn network marketing is by experience. You have to work network marketing to know network marketing.

The only exception is if you have a trusted friend who is experienced in network marketing and truly has your best interest at heart. Unfortunately, most people, even "friends" just want to get you into their company so that they can make money off of you. It might be a sad fact but in my experience it is true.

As you get going in network marketing, though, just keep in mind that the industry is definitely moving more and more toward automated phone fax systems. Until you actually try a particular system and have great success with it, don't believe anyone who says they have such a system perfected.

Television Commercials

Another aspect of the trend toward automation of prospect-gathering is that now there are generic T.V. commercials for getting leads. These generic commercials about "working at home" are tied to an 800#, and are provided distributors by the company. Due to the higher cost of producing (or purchasing) such commercials, the videos are rarely given away free, and when they are run on local television stations it is from a "broadcast" quality and larger format tape than the one you run in your home VCR. So expect to pay more for such pre-packaged commercials.

On the positive side, you can now get a telecommunication or voice mail company to answer all these leads and input the person's name, address and phone. They will then fax these leads to you, and all you have to do is send out either a postcard or other information referring these prospects to another 800# that provides all the information mentioned above. In other words, you're using mass media to drive people toward the more specific media of a phone/fax system. I expect that, as this way of gathering names progresses, it will be more common than not for companies to e-mail prospect information in tab delimited or comma delimited text files which can then be imported directly into a database on your computer for use with you word processing or e-mail program. Or they'll mail you a diskette.

Some companies now even offer a trained sales staff to close these leads for you. From what I can tell, much of network marketing is moving towards simply a monetary investment. You get involved, write your check, and then let the company or your upline do everything for you.

Of course this is the ideal that everyone wants—you just put in a certain amount of money and get that multiplied back to you in far greater numbers. It's sort of like the lottery, network marketing–style, because it is much, much easier said than done. Think about it. Let's say you have some money to invest and you're thinking about getting into one of these "we do it all for you" systems. The very obvious question is why do they need your investment, if the operation is in place and working so well? And if the system works so well, why do they need anyone to mail postcards? You pay for running the commercial, they fax you the leads that result, and then you mail out the postcards. If it's such a money-maker, why should they include you in the picture at all? Why not invest their own money, keep the leads, and pay minimum wage to some teenager or retired person to mail out the postcards?

The answer is, most of the time any system advertised as sure fire and foolproof simply does not work the way it is supposed to work.

That is precisely why, with all the marvelous technology available today, some of the best network marketers are those who are willing to talk to people.

As you know, I do not like to sell or twist anyone's arm. I succeeded because I combined a simple unobtrusive system of contacting people already interested in network marketing with a new pay plan that worked so well all I had to do was answer questions. Even though I never made any outgoing "sales calls" when my Changes business was really taking off, I was on the phone all day long. But when I was on the phone, I never overtly tried to sell anyone. I just answered questions. If they were not interested that was OK. When you do that long enough, and you're certain about your pay plan and your products, you know that in the end it is simply a numbers game. There are a certain percentage of people who will hear the truth in what you are saying and get involved, and they will in turn find other people of like mind. The better your system and the better your pay plan for the average person—and I emphasize the average person—the better off you will be and the more money you will make. It's that simple.

Using the Internet.

I mentioned e-mail earlier. One of my distributors uses the Internet frequently. I do not. I wish I could report to you that he has e-mailed thousands of people about the Changes International opportunity and received tremendous response, but it simply has not happened. He has told me that even though he is on the computer quite a bit and advertises a lot, he still gets only a small percentage of his people this way. It will probably become more effective in the future as more people become familiar with the Internet, just as it took time for people to get used to phones and faxes. It really hasn't been that long since having a VCR in your home was a very expensive proposition. When the cost of VCRs came down to a few hundred dollars, then you started seeing them everywhere. I think that when the same thing happens with computers, more people will be using e-mail and Websites than not, but right now it simply isn't the norm.

We are working on a generic Changes Website, which hopefully will have a similar effect to the generic television commercial mentioned earlier. After all, who wouldn't like to have a Website you could list on a business card (or a postcard left laying around a store the way I described in an earlier chapter). Then someone could surf to your site, read what they wanted, or download it for offline reading, and make a decision about getting involved. Of course, they could also see onscreen interactive comparisons of other marketing plans, see video testimonials of enthusiastic distributors, and place an order right there online with a 128-bit encrypted secure browser. It really makes a lot of sense, when you think about it. (Just because I'm not using it much right now doesn't mean I don't know about it!)

When Twin Labs acquired Changes, they invested many thousands of dollars in hardware and software upgrades, so even Changes has gone through quite a bit of change themselves lately!

If You Use The Internet

There are many ways to use the Internet to let people know about your network marketing opportunity. If you've been online a while, you might already have an e-mail database of several hundred people. If you have such a list, however, you've probably discovered that they don't like to get e-mail in which they see several hundred other people listed! So you have to figure out a way to reach them all in a way they find comfortable.

You can also market to people via Usenet newsgroups. You'll need the right software to read and post to these online groups, which numbered almost 40,000 as this was written. Send messages only to appropriate groups, like alt.business.opportunities. If you try to mail the same message to every group you find, you might soon find your e-mailbox so full of angry messages (known as "flames") that you'll spend all day just deleting them.

On the other hand, if you read messages that are posted by network marketers like yourself and then re-mail to them, it might work the same way it worked for me when I re-mailed to people who sent me opportunity offers in the mail. Another thing I suggest is that you use some cyber-shorthand to show that you're marketing something. This is Internet etiquette also known as Netiquette. For example:

ANN: Serious Moneymaking Opportunity

The ANN is shorthand for Announcement. And if you don't know, try not to use ALL CAPS on the Internet unless it's necessary, because it is perceived as the cyber-equivalent of shouting.

There are lots of Websites for magazines and other things that are pertinent to network marketing–type opportunities. You'll just have to visit Yahoo! or use Internet search engines to find them all. You can even fax people via the Internet at a cheaper price than regular phone lines. Whatever you do along this line, I wish you luck, and maybe I'll see you in cyberspace.

And Your Future Is?

For now, I'm putting the finishing touches on a whole new system and so, the signs are great. But I'd like to hear from you about any innovations you discover, on the Internet or in the real world.

My message remains the same. I am quite positive that any normal person can make good money in network marketing—at least a healthy part-time income—if they get with the right company, like I did with Changes International. If the pay plan is right, if the products are good, if you can keep a good balance in your life and not work yourself into oblivion, if you maintain a good positive mental outlook and share your enthusiasm with the people in the organization, and if you do everything humanly possible to support the efforts of the people in your downline, I simply don't see how you can fail. Network marketing is the best, perhaps even the only way that I know of, which allows a ten-time loser like me to prosper at a time in my life when most people would have long ago given up and called it a wash.

So many books on success talk about principles and leave out the specifics. That is why, in this book, I have covered a lot of the specifics of what happened in my life.

Having done that, I do feel it is important to review some of the most important principles. Because the principles that stand behind you might cause or initiate the specific thing you need to succeed. So here are what I believe are the basic principles behind success in network marketing.

BELIEF
You must believe that it is possible for YOU to make a lot of money. You must have this conviction. If you do not have it, the only way I know to get it is to brainwash your mind with success books and tapes.

DESIRE

You have to really want success. It cannot be a part time issue, at least not in your mind. You might have to start the business part time but the desire must be full time in your mind.

YOU MUST BE WILLING TO FAIL

While the other two principles apply to success in almost anything, this principle seems to apply in network marketing more than any thing else. Failure is actually a part of success, if you use the failure as a learning experience and not an emotional experience.

I think one common ingredient to all successful network marketers is that we are all **ETERNAL OPTIMISTS**. You have to be an optimist, because you will make mistakes and you will fail. If you get your feelings hurt and "take your marbles and go home" you will never make it. You must be willing to look at your failures as something to learn from.

The more you fail, the more you can learn. The more you learn, the higher your chances are of succeeding the next time.

Many things have changed in the network marketing business since January, 1995. Changes International has grown to be a major influence on the market, thanks in large part to the many positive benefits of Twin Labs and their continual efforts to make the company more professional in every way.

Similarly, I have had to change my marketing approach. Any business that wants to keep growing must learn to adapt. But that keeps life interesting.

I am still receiving those nice big checks, and that is the magic of network marketing.

I think it is only fitting to end this book with the first few sentences of that little booklet I wrote a few years ago that changed my life and the life of so many others:

"Network Marketing is truly one of the original golden opportunities of our time. No other vehicle can enable an individual without formal training to earn such vast sums of money. The are multiple thousands of people today who earn a six figure or more annual income through Network Marketing. Many of these don't even have high school diplomas."

Will you be next? I wish you all the best, and I'd love to hear from you.

Additional copies of *How a Shy Guy Like Me Earned Over $1 MILLION IN NETWORK MARKETING* are available from:

BOOKMASTERS
P.O. Box 388, Ashland, OH 44805
Order Phone: (800) 247-6553
Order Fax: (419) 281-6883
E-Mail: order@bookmaster.com
Website: www.bookmasters.com

❖   ❖   ❖

$22.95 for hardbound edition, plus $4.00 shipping for first copy ($1.50 each additional copy) and sales tax for CA and OH orders.

❖   ❖   ❖

You may contact JOE BROWN at:

L & L MANAGEMENT
c/o 556 S. Fair Oaks, #101-169
Pasadena, California PZ [91105]
Fax: (626) 568-9165